Presenting Magically

Transforming Your Stage Presence With NLP

Tad James MS, PhD
& David Shephard BSc, DES

Crown House Publishing Limited
www.crownhouse.co.uk

First published by

Crown House Publishing Ltd
Crown Buildings, Bancyfelin, Carmarthen, Wales, SA33 5ND, UK
www.crownhouse.co.uk

and

Crown House Publishing Company LLC
PO Box 2223, Williston, VT 05495, USA
www.crownhousepublishing.com

First published in hardback in 2001 (ISBN: 9781899836529).
Published in paperback and transferred to digital printing 2016.

British Library of Cataloguing-in-Publication Data
A catalogue entry for this book is available
from the British Library.

Paperback ISBN 978-178583156-0
Hardback ISBN 978-189983652-9
Mobi ISBN 978-184590246-9
ePub ISBN 978-184590354-1

LCCN 200211348

Table of Contents

Foreword

How many times have you left a presentation or training saying to yourself, "Wow, that was great. I wish I could do that! Why can't I be that good?"?

Thanks to Master Trainers Tad James and David Shephard, now you can. *Presenting Magically* is a compelling and beautifully written guide to effective communication and training excellence. In it, Tad and David depict the power of congruent communication in training by providing carefully chosen, easily understood and specific steps for enhancing your training skills to get the most fulfillment and success in your personal and professional life.

Communication is imperative to training. The quality of our communication largely determines the quality of our trainings—and our lives. Our communication is constant, whether or not we are speaking. We all, in one way or another, send our messages out to the world, and rarely do we send them consciously. We act out our state of being with nonverbal body language. We lift one eyebrow for disbelief. We rub our noses for puzzlement. We clasp our arms to isolate ourselves or to protect ourselves. We shrug our shoulders for indifference, wink one eye for intimacy, tap our fingers for impatience, and slap our forehead for forgetfulness. The gestures are numerous, and while some are deliberate, many are mostly unconscious.

To present magically is to communicate masterfully.

In this book, you will find precise directions and skill-building exercises to direct you along the path to training excellence. The learning process for these 'magical' communication and training skills can be compared with the process for learning a foreign language. It takes time and practice for the skills to become automatic. At first you master words, phrases and ground rules. Suddenly, you can communicate with a child's vocabulary. You continue to learn and practice until you acquire fluency. With the mastery of your new skills, you feel the freedom to be more creative in what has become your second tongue.

Have you ever noticed that the most effective teachers and trainers are those with high energy and personal power? Are you aware that the same energy and power is available to you? A sixth century BC Chinese philosopher Lao Tzu wrote of such personal power in the classic *Tao Te Ching*. He characterized *Te* as the potential energy that comes from being in the right place at the right time in the right frame of mind. The early Chinese came to regard *Te* as stored energy or potentiality, something that exists, though sometimes dormant, in everyone. The skills you learn in this book will help you find and release that energy in yourself—your personal power—and allow you to 'present magically'.

Written by two of the great trainers of our time, *Presenting Magically* should be read as much for its insight into the nature of mental functioning as for its brilliant approach to the art of training. This book will be a useful resource for people everywhere seeking to enhance their own growth and effectiveness.

Be aware that each of us is more powerful and has more impact than we suspect. Here, Tad James and David Shephard have created amazingly simple techniques for accessing and cultivating this part of ourselves. I believe that using this personal power in a positive way can have personal, corporate, city, state and perhaps even national and global repercussions. Thanks to the excellent trainings that Tad and David have provided throughout the world, many people have already discovered their personal power and use it daily.

When you join them, you will find your trainings and energy moving to new levels, your interactions more satisfying and your work more meaningful. This is an important book, a true breakthrough in the field of communications and training. Study it well, and refer to it often. Do the exercises. *Presenting Magically* is the only training text you will ever need!

Caroline Miller, Ph.D.
Co-author, *Healing Yourself with Self-Hypnosis*

Introduction

We both came into training after various other jobs, such as selling and management consultancy, and it seemed that we had something to offer to other people. At the same time, we had been on the receiving end of much training, mostly of indifferent quality. However some of them stood out because there were some engaging and inspiring presenters who made everything entertaining, and did it with seemingly little effort. During such presentations, it was easy to wonder, "What is it that they are doing that is different, that makes them excellent presenters?" And then: "I want to do this. I'm sure these people weren't born doing it, so there must be a way of learning how to be this good. And I am willing to do whatever it takes to become an excellent trainer and presenter myself."

That journey led us to discover the basics of *Presenting Magically*, and, for 15 years we have been training the top trainers in Neuro-Linguistic Programming (NLP) in the world.

Overview

In this book we are going to be explaining what NLP is and what it has to offer in presentation skills. We presuppose that you know little or nothing about NLP. Essentially, NLP is more an attitude of mind rather than a set of techniques. It presents new ways of doing things, and fosters willingness to explore what could be. In other words, it is a way of expanding your own world of possibilities.

As we share this information with you, we will often include essential 'stage directions' and descriptions of what we are doing.

In a live training, we continually vary the pace and voice tonality with what is being said. Some of the examples . . . and some of the instructions . . . will work . . . much better . . . for you . . . if you read them s-l-o-w-l-y. However, in the main body of the text, we will be indicating pauses only where they are absolutely essential, or to make a point about pausing. Otherwise, the text would be full of dots . . .

For certain exercises, it would be better to listen to the words, either live or on tape. You could have someone read the text aloud to you, in the appropriate manner, or record it, and then listen to the tape so that you can do what is necessary with your body, or inside your head.

The secret

In this book, we will share a number of the 'trade secrets' of professional presenters, as well as top NLP trainers. There is more to this book than is immediately obvious. We all take language for granted most of the time. But when you understand how it works on an unconscious level, you can begin to use it to help get your message across. You will learn to recognise some of the language patterns by getting curious about, "Why is he saying that in this way?" "What is this bit really about?" "How does this work?" "What if I were to use that myself?" Some things won't be explained until we are well into the book, while others will not be explained at all. But they will have been happening.

Actually, the best way of hiding things is to . . . Are you familiar with Edgar Allan Poe's story *The Purloined Letter*? The police detective is looking for a very important letter. He has made an exhaustive and meticulous search of the flat, looking in all places that he thinks someone is likely to hide something. This is his downfall, because in fact, the missing letter is stuck in full view in the letter rack on the wall. So as you read, look again, and you will find many examples of what is being taught.

How to get the most out of this book

The structure of this book is similar to the training and follows the same sequence of exercises. The first six chapters establish the groundwork. Then we will start doing the exercises. We recommend that the first time through, you read each chapter and do the exercises in order, as each exercise builds on the ones before. To become an excellent presenter or trainer you do need to practise the skills. Then you will be getting direct evidence that what you are doing is making a difference.

The ideas in this book can be used immediately. Right from the first exercise you will have something to explore, and not just in formal settings. There will be many occasions when you can use these skills appropriately with anyone you are communicating with for whatever purpose. Presenting also includes talking one-on-one with family, friends and work colleagues.

In Chapter Fourteen we will be exploring four different learning styles. If you are the kind of person who immediately wants to get on and do the exercises – which is one of the learning styles – then please bear with us, because in order to accommodate other learning style preferences, we must first do the set-ups and framing for the book.

Having a structure is useful for achieving the best results. Therefore, we recommend that you:

- Allocate a regular amount of time for doing the reading, and for doing the exercises.
- Break the material into suitable-sized pieces according to the time available.
- Take breaks of five to ten minutes every hour or so, as this will aid your learning.
- Maintain your momentum by doing a number of exercises every day or every week, or by doing several during a weekend. By establishing a regular schedule for your learning, you will soon see changes in yourself and the results you are getting, and thus stay motivated.
- Find opportunities to use the material in your everyday life. If you can do some training or presenting, even better.

Forming working groups
Presenting is not a solitary activity. Ideally we would suggest that you work through this book with a group of like-minded people who also want to improve their presentation and training communication skills. The ideal group number is about five or six people, so that when you are doing an exercise in front of your group, the audience is large enough for you to observe that what you are doing is working for everyone. By learning together, you benefit from each other's experiences. You will also be developing your own skills in front of a real group, and you will be making this

learning part of your own style. Unfortunately, you will not be getting the feedback you would receive during a live training. However, a word of encouragement. People often say, "I am not sure whether I did the exercise right". We ask: "Did it work?" If they say, "Yes", we say, "You did it right". The result is the most important thing. (If you are already a trainer or presenter, and you are going to be working on your own through this book, then see Appendix A.)

In our trainings we suggest that in order for people to get the most out of the exercises they form a group with people they don't know. Then they have to make the effort to find out about those other people's preferences, and so on. At the end of the training they will know, "If it worked for these people whom I didn't know, then it will work for anybody". However, it is fine if you are doing this with people you know. In that case you will probably be surprised at what you discover about them that you did not consciously know before. It is our experience that in either case, most people are actually working with strangers!

● If you don't know everyone in the group, take this opportunity to introduce yourself, and to tell them a little bit about yourself. Maybe tell them some of your outcomes from reading *Presenting Magically*, so that they can support you in achieving those goals during your time together.

Putting on a training
If you are new to presenting, let us give you some of the basics around putting on a training such as *Presenting Magically*. Use a hotel that is familiar with such events. It means the essentials are provided and the staff members know what to do. Use a spacious room with raised staging at one end, with a couple of barstools and a flipchart. Around the room there will be sufficient chairs for the pre-booked participants, and a large 'break-out' space for doing exercises, also with chairs, so that you don't spend time moving furniture. You should provide your own sound system, so that you can use a microphone to be clearly heard by everyone and play music as well. Having your own system also enables you to make sound recordings of the training if you wish. Hotel sound systems are notoriously bad.

Stage-manage the whole event – make sure that the training room is completely ready before you allow the course participants to enter. When they do come in, there will be music playing. This means that they will be coming into a different space, probably unlike the usual training room, and this will immediately alert them that, 'something different is happening here'. This is the kind of state to have the audience in at the beginning. This creates for them a sense of moving into the unknown, where anything might happen.

Chapter One
Setting the Frame

Introducing . . .

How do you start a training or a presentation? There are many possibilities. Doubtless you will find your own unique way of beginning. Here as an example is the way we do it. When everyone is settled, stand at centre stage, and start by saying something like this:

"Good morning. How are you feeling? Are you ready for this? Whatever 'this' is, by the way. What are we actually doing today? *Presenting Magically* is what we are doing. And it sounds from talking to a number of you outside . . . Oh, by the way, for those of you who haven't met me before, let me tell you my name. I am _____. It is great to meet you all. We have a very good, exciting three days planned, and you will be seeing quite a lot of me, and our assistants. We will be watching you as you are presenting, over these days. So it's looking good. Let me give you the big picture of what *Presenting Magically* is about, just in case you don't know, so that you can decide whether you do really want to be here."

Now this introduction may seem a little strange, rather contrived, but there are reasons for this, which we'll go over later, but only after we have covered many other things.

Presenting Magically is about your being totally comfortable and congruent, being yourself, in front of an audience of any size. And however many people there are in that audience – one person, a dozen people, or 1000 people – you are presenting or training to great effect, remaining totally at ease in front of them.

When you make the techniques and skills in this book your own, you will be able to connect with every single person in an audience of any size so that they all feel a very strong connection with you. Then you will have their full attention for the whole period of time. And this means that you will be able to communicate so effectively to a group that everyone in the group gets your message and derives the highest possible level of learning from your presentation or training.

The key phrase is *being comfortable, being yourself*. Because as we were preparing this training, we were amazed at how many professional presenters and trainers said:

"I can't be me in front of an audience. First I have to put on my 'presentation suit'. And I adopt a special presentation personality for use in these situations."

So we asked:

"Well, wouldn't it be a lot easier if you were just you?"
"Oh no, I couldn't just be myself in front of an audience. That wouldn't be powerful enough. I have to have my 'armour' on."

Most likely what they weren't saying was:

"Because if I don't have my presentation armour then I would feel weak, or vulnerable, or open to attack."

Presenting Magically is about leaving the armour behind, allowing yourself to come out from behind your wall, and being totally comfortable and being totally OK being yourself in front of an audience. Any audience. And by the end of this book, having done all the exercises, this is what you can expect to be doing. That would be a skill well worth having, wouldn't it?

Why are you here?
Having explained the overall purpose of the training, you need to bring everybody into the group, so that they are totally focused on what you have to tell them. When people first arrive at a training, when they walk in the door, you have no idea what has just been

happening to them. If they have been travelling, and the traffic was bad or the train was late, their journey may have put them in an agitated state. They may have left home having had an argument with some member of the family. Or they may consider that attending the training is 'having a few days off', 'a holiday' from the office, from the project they are engaged in, or away from their demanding customers, or whatever. And some of them will definitely be there to hear what you have to say, and can't wait to get the goodies!

Whatever state people arrive in, you need to make sure that, if it is less than ideal for learning, you can move them into a state that is more useful for getting what you are offering. A good way of doing that is to have them focus on their reasons for being there.

Ask them to direct their attention away from their immediate past experience, out into the future, toward what they want, or hope to gain personally. You may say something like:

> "So, why are you here? Whenever I have a group of people with me, I presuppose that they have some reason for being here. Because if you don't have a reason for being here, you would be somewhere else, wouldn't you? So what are your personal reasons for being here? Why bother to do this training?

> "It might be because you have had some experiences of presenting or training in the past, or of being up in front of an audience, which maybe didn't go quite as well as you would have liked. Or maybe it went OK, but you thought, 'I can do better, out in the future.'

> "Maybe your current situation means you are having to do more presentations than before. Or you have to do them now, but you have never done any presenting before. Or maybe you have been asked to do some trainings, to train some other people, and you want to find out how to do that.

> "Or maybe there are things you are wanting to do in the future. Maybe you want to become a presenter or a trainer, or you want to work with groups of people – doing sales presentations, business presentations, or general public training."

Take a moment to review your reasons for reading this book. And whatever your reasons are, that's fine. They are your reasons. And you can change them, or add to them whenever you wish.

The number one fear

Many people have some kind of strong response to the thought of presenting in public. When a survey was done in the United States, asking people what they were most afraid of, public speaking was at the top of the list. Public speaking is the number one fear in the United States. The number two fear in the US is death. So you could say that, in the States, there are more people who are afraid of speaking in front of an audience than are afraid of dying. Here in the United Kingdom, public speaking comes in at number two on the chart of fears. The number one fear in the UK is fear of spiders. Then comes public speaking. If you were speaking in front of a group of spiders then it would rise to number one. But generally it comes second.

Even well-known people that we might assume would be totally OK in front of an audience, such as actors and performers who do it for a living, may still have this fear before they go on stage. For example, the actor Jimmy Durante, who was famous in the 40s and 50s, and whose last film was, *It's a Mad, Mad, Mad, Mad World* (1963) had terrible stage fright. Even though Jimmy 'Schnozzola' Durante spent his life on the stage, in the movies, and making public appearances, one thing that is not well known is that he was so afraid of being in front of an audience, that he physically threw up before each time he went on stage or did a public presentation. He was physically sick because he was so nervous about performing. So if you are feeling in any way less than totally cool, calm and relaxed about 'presentations!' – like *"Eerrgh!"* or *"Help!"* – then know you are in good company.

One of the things that we can guarantee the people who come on the live trainings is that by the end of the first day, all of their performance anxiety around presentation will have totally disappeared. For most people this happens easily, although a few may need some personal attention. However, without the direct contact, all we can do in this book is take you through some processes that will definitely help you let go of any fears, nervousness, or limiting beliefs that you have about yourself, which concern your being less than totally magnificent and powerful in front of an audience. When these fears have disappeared you can then enjoy the rest of the exercises and get the most out of this book.

For the moment, continue to mull over your personal reasons for reading this book. And while you are thinking about them, let us tell you about the practical considerations of doing a training or presentation.

Time integrity

In a training, it is important to keep to a certain time frame, because there is a lot to fit in. Explain the timing schedule right at the start, so that the audience knows what is expected.

Training agreements

To ensure the smooth running of the training, you must get some agreements from the course participants. Agreeing to these things means that we will more easily achieve the results we want. Ask participants to:

- *Be on time,* both at the beginning of the day, and after each break.
- *Turn off mobile phones and pagers* – or at least put them on vibrate mode.
- *Keep all conversations front to back.* Which means that during the training, all conversations involve the trainer or presenter and just one person in the audience – rather than there being separate conversations taking place all over the room.
- Make sure that all of your *attention* is on what is happening *at the front* of the room, because that will enable you to get the most out of the training.

Conscious unconscious integration

One of the major differences between what we do and what happens during other trainings is that the content is designed to enable people to learn both with their conscious and with their unconscious mind. Therefore, all behaviour in a training is intentional and designed to work on both levels.

In learning *Presenting Magically* you will be doing many exercises. To get the most out of them you need to engage in them fully, and do them to the very best of your ability. As you work through them, you will find that you are soon doing so much that you get consciously overloaded. From our side, this is intentional. The material is challenging, because it is new and different, and you have so much to concentrate on that you will no longer be able to think consciously. Then you will have to trust your unconscious mind. After all, that is where learning is really happening.

Previous experience of NLP
Much of the material in this book is based on concepts from NLP, which will be explained in Chapter Two. Our introductory trainings invariably have people new to NLP in them. The good thing about NLP is that you start from where you are. No previous knowledge is required.

Exercise 1: Your Goals and Outcomes

One significant finding coming from Neuro-Linguistic Programming is that you achieve far better results when you start with the end in mind, when you are clear about your reasons for wanting to achieve your goals and outcomes.

Therefore it is worth spending the time at the beginning of a project – such as working through *Presenting Magically* – to write down your personal reasons for reading this book, your reasons for wanting to be an excellent trainer or presenter. Actually commit them to paper. You don't have to share them with anyone else, except maybe with the people in your practice group.

But just before you do write them down, consider this:

People often tell us that they think we are greedy, because when we go on a training, when we set goals and reasons for being there, the question we ask is:

> "What would my reasons for being here have to be, such that, by the end of the training, if all of my reasons were satisfied, I would have to say to myself: 'That was the very best training I have ever been on in my life so far'?"

So regarding your reading of this book:

> "What would your goals have to be, such that when you finish the book, having done all the exercises, and having achieved all of those goals, you would say: 'That was the best training book I have ever read on developing myself and my skills.'?"

By thinking that way, you dramatically increase the probability of getting it all. And really we want you to get more out of this training than you ever dreamed you could get out of the book when you first opened it.

Take five minutes and write down your reasons and goals for being here.

Do this exercise now.

What are your goals and outcomes for reading this book?
Write down your reasons, your outcomes and goals below and overleaf. You can always add to your list. As you get further into the book you may think of things that you weren't aware of when you started. When that happens, put them on your list.

Chapter Two
Neuro-Linguistic Programming

Neuro-Linguistic Programming is the underlying set of principles behind what we do in our *Presenting Magically* trainings. Even if you already know about NLP, getting another description is always interesting and useful, because each new explanation offers some new learning, or an understanding at a deeper level.

NLP is not a complete body of knowledge, since it is always growing. The creators of NLP, Richard Bandler and John Grinder, in the mid-1970s, referred to NLP as, "An attitude, and a methodology that leaves behind a trail of techniques". That may not immediately make a lot of sense, so we need to explore what it means.

Attitude
The essential attitude is one of *curiosity*. If you have ever seen someone doing something so expertly, so skilfully, and been so impressed by it that you wanted to be able to do the same thing as well, then you will have probably asked yourself the question: "How do they do that?"

- Maybe you enjoy a certain presenter, and you start wondering, "How are they making that presentation so much fun?"
- Maybe you were engrossed by an engaging trainer and thought, "Why are they so captivating? What are they doing that's different?"
- In a sales presentation you experienced someone getting a tremendous response, and you want to know how to achieve that too.
- Perhaps you encountered an educator or a personal development trainer with a wonderful way of handling audiences, and you would like to have similar success.

Curiosity is asking: "How do they do that? How do I get those kinds of results?" You may even start asking them questions because you want to find out how they do what they do. This is the kind of curiosity we're talking about.

In *Presenting Magically* you will encounter things that you have not seen other presenters or trainers doing before. If you start getting curious about, "Why are they doing that?" or, "What do you have to do? How does this work? And what would happen in my trainings or presentations if I were to start doing these things?" then you will be getting some answers.

Wanton experimentation

You also need to engage in *wanton experimentation*. That word 'wanton' is important. It means you have to have the willingness to do anything, just to find out what would happen if you did it. Are you willing to keep trying different things, to find out what is going to get you the results you want?

You are going to be doing things you have never done before, so there is no way for you to know ahead of time what would happen if you did them. Over the years we have observed that people get extremely varied results when doing these exercises. So we cannot predict specifically what will happen for you. If in an exercise you are feeling a little hesitant: "I'm not sure if I can do that", or, "I have never done anything like that before", then we would suggest that you simply take to heart the words from that great American 'philosopher' Nike, and *"Just do it"*, and find out what happens.

The creators of NLP were curious about several people who were excellent in their own field, and found out exactly what they were doing that made a difference. They modeled hypnotherapist Milton Erickson (1901-80), family therapist Virginia Satir (1916-88) and also Fritz Perls (1893-1970), who was the charismatic creator of Gestalt therapy. Fortunately there were many films of him working with clients. One thing Fritz Perls said has become a kind of talisman for us, and we suggest you consider this when you are doing an exercise. Fritz would often say to the people he was working with: "Stop thinking, and come to your senses."

We have designed the exercises in *Presenting Magically* to be cumulative for the reader. Soon you will have so many things to pay attention to in an exercise that you won't be able consciously to hold everything in your mind. So then: stop thinking, come to your senses, and just do it. That is one of our guidelines for excelling in the exercises. By just doing it, you will find you have abilities you didn't even realise you have, abilities you can then use to ever greater benefit.

Methodology

The foundation of NLP is a methodology called *modeling*, which Richard Bandler and John Grinder used for finding out what Milton Erickson, Fritz Perls, and also the family therapist, Virginia Satir, did when they were working with clients. (We will meet Virginia Satir again in Chapter Thirteen, when we come to non-verbal communication.) Basically, with modeling, you find people who are examples of excellence, observe what they do, ask them questions, and see if by doing the same things you can get the same result.

Briefly, to model someone, you may observe:

- their physiology, what that person does with their body
- the language they use, how they use words, how they structure their utterances to get results
- their thinking, how they construct their models of reality.

The remarkable thing is that if you adopt the same physiology, use language in the same way, and structure your thinking in the same way, then you will get very similar results to those of the expert you are modeling.

We do not claim that NLP is new. Similar ideas occur throughout history. For example, to return to Poe's story, *The Purloined Letter*, published in 1844, one character says:

> "When I wish to find out how wise, or how stupid, or how good, or how wicked is any one, or what are his thoughts at the moment, I fashion the expression of my face, as accurately as possible, in accordance with the expression of his, and then wait

> to see what thoughts or sentiments arise in my mind or heart, as
> if to match or correspond with the expression."

Much work has been done in modeling excellent presenters and trainers, but *Presenting Magically* gives you the practical *how-to's*, which means that anyone who wishes to achieve excellent results can do what has been found to work consistently well. We will share with you some models of how to use your physiology, how to structure your language, as well as your thinking. If you practise the material in this book, then by the end of the book you will know that you are an excellent presenter and trainer. You won't just know it theoretically. You will know it experientially, because you will have been in front of an audience doing it. And you will probably be surprised at how well you did it.

Techniques

NLP is more than just learning some techniques that you add to what you already know. Doing NLP means changing how you think. Just giving you techniques would be selling you short. Remember that saying: "If I give you a fish, then I feed you for a day. If I teach you how to fish, then I feed you for life." We want to teach you how to fish. We want to enable you to change your life, by changing the way you think, so that you become totally comfortable being yourself and more flexible in what you are doing when you are in front of an audience.

Now changing your way of thinking is not something you do just by thinking about it! It happens when you fully experience doing some activity, involving your body and mind, your language and your behaviour. So let's explore in more detail how an understanding of NLP will help you achieve this. We'll begin by considering its three component parts.

Neuro
Neuro refers to the nervous system, your neurology, your brain. It includes all of your senses: seeing, hearing, touching, smelling, and tasting. Every second, approximately two million bits of

information are flooding into your nervous system, even when you are asleep.

Inside, you make sense of that information by representing it to yourself: you create pictures inside your head; you hear sounds inside; you have feelings, even smells and tastes inside. You also talk to yourself about it inside your head. Most people have internal dialogues or conversations with themselves. When you are talking to yourself, do you say useful things to yourself? Or do you talk to yourself in a limiting way? For example: "You can't do that! You must be kidding."

There are at least six things going on inside your head. If you were to stop right now, and check what you are doing inside, you would find one of more of those activities happening. Indeed, if you are not doing any of those things, check for a pulse!

These *internal representations* in our neurology form our *model of the world*. This is how we make sense of neural activity, how we communicate to ourselves and others, how we explain what things mean. The language we use affects our internal representations, and the meaning of those internal representations determines how we behave.

Linguistic
It is obvious that the language we use affects other people's behaviour. This is more than their compliance with our actual words. Saying to someone, "I want to know how you do what you do", "What you did was excellent", or "I'm going to tell you a secret" will affect the state they are in, as well as what they are likely to do as a consequence.

This applies in any context. For example, if you are giving a sales presentation, the language you use will affect the state and behaviour of your prospective clients. Curiosity would lead you to want to know how to affect the prospective clients' state and behaviour in such a way that they will buy from you, that they will sign the contract – since that is the outcome of a successful sales presentation.

The purpose of any presentation is to get your message across. The way you are communicating when you are presenting or training – what you say and how you say it – will be affecting the state and potential behaviour of everyone in the audience. Therefore, to get your message across easily and effectively, you need to know how to structure your communication so that every single person in the room is in the best state for receiving your message. That way you get the result you want, and at the same time they learn the things they want.

Programming
Since we've both done computer programming, when we first encountered NLP, it was the *programming* part that attracted our attention. We wondered: "Does this literally mean you can reprogram people? ... Maybe you could get a keyboard and plug it into the back of your head and with a few keystrokes ... " Because, "I have some stuff that I would like to reprogram. I run several programs that don't really work. And I can certainly think of some other people I would like to reprogram!"

The 'programming' in NLP is actually more subtle, and refers to our habits, our repeating patterns of thinking and behaving. These programs are running unconsciously, which is why we aren't usually aware of them. For example, we run programs for getting up in the morning, and programs for not getting up in the morning. We have programs for getting excited, programs for getting motivated, programs for making decisions, programs for learning, programs for being creative, programs for knowing what is real, and programs for remembering. Some of them work effectively; others may be less than effective. Sometimes we achieve our own programming, sometimes we have programming thrust upon us – by parents, teachers, and others. What is important is discovering and using programs that consistently work well and achieve excellence.

One of the purposes of this book is to give you some new programs that will help you achieve your specific desires and outcomes. We hope to assist and enable you to totally transform your stage presence, and the way you communicate so that you are a magnificent presenter or trainer.

The NLP communication model

NLP is essentially how you communicate effectively, both with yourself and with other people. From an NLP perspective, this is what happens within someone's neurology when they are on the receiving end of our communication *(Figure 2.1)*:

Figure 2.1

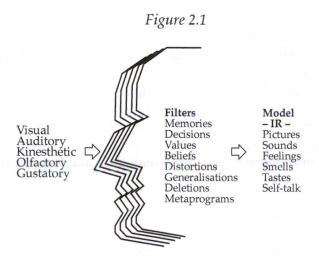

Take a pen and draw a box round the list of words on the left hand side, in a colour of your choice, where it says, 'Visual, auditory, kinesthetic, olfactory, gustatory'. When you have drawn the box round them, label it: 'External event or communication.'

NLP has its own jargon – technical-sounding words that have simple meanings. We will do our best to 'dejargonise' it. We will also teach you the jargon, as it might be useful if you are talking to NLP people. But, with a name like 'Neuro-Linguistic Programming', you probably assumed that it was going to have jargon in it. For example, those words for the five senses:

- Visual = see
- Auditory = hear
- Kinesthetic = feel
- Olfactory = smell
- Gustatory = taste

Figure 2.1 shows a schematic of the communication process. Information about events on the outside comes into our neurology through our five senses. Two million bits of information is a massive amount to be arriving in the nervous system every second of the day. In order to keep us from perpetual overload, we employ three processes to cope with all this information: *deletion, generalisation,* and *distortion.*

Deletion

What would happen if we were consciously aware of all that information? Our thinking would be so excessively burdened that we wouldn't be able to process any of it, and very likely we would go insane. But this doesn't happen, because we limit our awareness and deal with only what is important to us at the time. We select certain parts of the incoming information to pay attention to, and filter out everything else. It is as though we are ignoring everything we consider irrelevant, and that information gets *deleted* from conscious awareness.

For example, these experiences are common:

- You are so deeply engaged in reading a book or the newspaper, that you are oblivious to somebody asking you a question.
- You are looking for your car keys, and you can't find them anywhere. Then you discover they have been right in front of you all the time.
- Notice how the clothes you are wearing at the moment feel against your skin. Most of the time these body sensations are totally ignored.

The information is coming in through your eyes, your ears, and your skin all the time, but for whatever reason your conscious mind deletes it, until you start paying attention to it.

Generalisation

We also reduce the amount of information we are dealing with by generalising it. Human beings are very good at noticing patterns, regularities, and creating abstract principles and rules. Words are labels for categories of experience. Generalising allows us to recognise classes of objects, such as chairs and pens, even though their physical appearance can vary enormously. Even names for individual people are generalisations over time. Tad James and David Shephard in 1986 are taken to be the same Tad James and David Shephard in 2001, even though every cell in our bodies has changed in that time.

Generalising also enables us to reasonably forecast what is likely to happen. For example, scientific knowledge is the collection of general principles that tell us how the universe works, and allow us to make predictions. We don't need to relearn how to drive each time we get into a different car. Although cars vary in the layout of the controls – so that instead of indicating turning right, you turn on the windscreen wipers! – in general, they work in the same way. They have similar arrangements of engine, steering wheel, accelerator and so on. Even though the engine design and external appearance may vary greatly, the *functions* stay constant.

We condense vast amounts of information about the world into useful 'facts'. In the Introduction we referred to the number one fear and saying that, "In the US . . . " It is a useful generalisation, because it has meaning for us, but it is only a *statistical* fact. If you were to ask any particular American citizen, then they may or may not have that fear.

We also generalise our own experiences. For example, someone may have done a single presentation during which the audience was aggressive, they didn't know what to do, and they felt awful. Based on that one experience, they now decide that all audiences are hostile and that they are no good at presenting. They are generalising from certain aspects of their experience and assuming that in the future every presentation will be the same. We frequently do a mental operation that changes our description of an external experience into an internal assessment of our *identity*: "That was an awful presentation", becomes, "*I* am no good at presenting". This is often a less than useful inference.

Opening the door
We actually learn everything through generalising. For example: From your early learning experiences, you have inferred certain rules about the way doors work. Most domestic doors have hinges on one side, which allow the door to swing open or shut,

and you usually need to turn a handle in order to release the catch.

Some investigators once did an experiment with an unconventional door (*Figure* 2.2). This door had a handle on the *same* side as the hinge. The hinge would still allow the door to move freely, such that if you pushed it on the opposite side, it would swing open. They said to the victims: "Here is a special challenge for you. Open the door, and get to the other side."

Figure 2.2

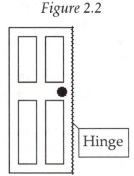

The first thing most people do, using their usual generalisations, is to turn the door handle. But the door doesn't open. They try turning it the other way. Still no joy. Then they push and they pull where the handle is, but still it doesn't open.

Then they leap to the conclusion that the door must be locked, and ask for the key. But even when they unlock the door, it still doesn't work. At this point in the exercise, most people say the door must be jammed and that it is impossible to open it. They have reached the limit of their generalising.

It is only possible to open the door by going beyond the well-known rules 'known' about doors. Apparently one guy, after twenty minutes, did get through the door, but probably by saying, "Oh, I give up!" and leaning on the far edge of the door, so it swung open.

Having generalisations about the way everything works simplifies the amount of information we need to pay attention to. Most of the time, in familiar contexts, these generalisations work for us. However, there will be other contexts where they don't work, and we then have to go back to first principles, and reconsider what to do with the raw information.

Distortion
We also distort information. We make connections between what we perceive, and what it might mean, or what might happen as a

result. We are distorting information by labelling experiences in the world around us, interpreting them, making meaning, drawing inferences, and coming to conclusions. For example:

- "When I look at the people in the room, I know we're going to have a good time."
- "They're not back from the exercise yet, so they must be finding it interesting."
- "I'll give them lots of handouts, because that will keep them happy."
- "If I learn this technique, everything will be much easier in the future."

David remembers:

"When I was about 16 years old, my parents went away for the weekend. They had decided I was old enough to stay in the house by myself. I was really excited about this, because I had never been left to look after the house before. So I got some beers, stayed up watching television until two in the morning – all the sort of things you do when you are feeling 'Yes!! I'm free! I'm an adult'. I went to bed around two o'clock, and then woke up at three o'clock, because I heard some noises. It was the sound of someone moving around downstairs, and my heart started almost leaping out of my chest. So what do you do? The first thing is to pull the covers over your head, because then you will be safe! Nobody will guess you are there!

"By this time I could hear footsteps coming up the stairs and begin walking along the landing outside my room. My heart was still pounding away, and I was thinking, 'Well, there is only one way of handling this. I have to catch this person by surprise'. The best thing I could think of, as far as surprises are concerned, was to stand behind my bedroom door, with my baseball bat. So I was standing there behind the door. The steps were getting closer . . . Until the point came where I thought that this person was right outside the door. I flung the door open, 'Wah!!' and leaped through the doorway to catch them by surprise . . .

"That's right, there was nobody there. And there never had been anybody there. It was the sound of the central heating system cooling down, making that knocking sound. And it was always the central heating system cooling down. But in my brain I had

19

distorted the incoming auditory information and made it mean something completely different. In so doing I had changed my physiological state, so that adrenalin was now coursing through my body, and my heart was thumping away."

Beliefs

We also distort incoming information through our beliefs. Whatever your beliefs are, in the face of conflicting information, you will most likely justify them and insist on your truth. Consider this: Have you ever had a conversation with someone who has some very strongly-held beliefs, and you provide them with a massive amount of information which is contrary to their beliefs, and they say, "You're right. You are totally correct in what you are saying. How could I have been so stupid! I'll immediately change my mind on this!" That doesn't happen, does it? People will resist any outside attempts to change their beliefs and keep those beliefs intact by filtering out any contradictory evidence.

Here is an example of this phenomenon. Suppose you have a belief that you are not an excellent presenter. Now even if you are an absolutely brilliant presenter, you will create situations that prove your belief to be correct. Perhaps you get up on stage and do a great presentation, but you think that you haven't, because you believe you aren't a great presenter. Then someone in the audience comes up to you and says, "You know, that was a great presentation". You say, "Oh, thanks very much". But as you walk away you are thinking, "Oh, they are only saying that to be nice". You have to do this, otherwise your belief would be blown out.

Many beliefs tend to operate in the background, and we don't always know what they are. So think back to when you were presenting. Pretend that you are watching yourself from the side of the stage. And notice your own response to how you are doing. How do you respond to that 'you' giving the presentation? Pay close attention to your response. You may notice that you are doing OK, or that you could be doing better in some way. Once you bring your beliefs out into the open by acknowledging your response to your presentation, you can begin to improve your future presentations. You can simply let go of any limiting beliefs, and allow yourself to become a truly great presenter.

Our Model of the World

Our 'model of the world' is exactly that. It is how we make sense of all our experiences: the pictures, sounds, feelings, smells, tastes and self-talk. We update our model of the world as we select or filter the information coming in, according to our outcomes – what we want; to our beliefs – about the way things are, how things work; and to our values – what is important to us. Our outcomes, beliefs and values change over time, and we are continually re-creating our model of the world on the basis of current information and current filters and interpretations.

Negatives

When the human brain is creating an internal representation, it cannot directly represent a negative concept. So if we say: "Don't think of a blue tree," you immediately think of a blue tree. You may then engage in a secondary activity that allows you somehow to negate that image, but this can happen only after you have first invoked what you are not supposed to be thinking of. So you can't not think of something you are not supposed to be thinking about without thinking about it. So don't even think about that for a moment!

When you listen to the content of many presentations and trainings, you often hear words that describe exactly what you are not supposed to think and do. One thing we have noticed, especially in sales presentations, is that most of the objections that arise are ones the presenter suggested!

An example of this was a presentation Tad went to, put on by two financial companies, both offering new investment packages. They were going for the same section of the market, and both had created investment deals for people who wanted their money to be particularly safe, with a reasonable return. At the launching of these new products, there were about 45 people in the room who were either customers or people who would be selling the products. Here is what happened. We will indicate the emphasis by putting the important words in italics.

21

The presenter from the first company came on stage and said:

> "I would like to introduce you to our new product. With this par-
> ticular product we don't want to put all of your money *at risk*.
> The most important thing is we really want to make sure that
> you don't *lose all of your money*."

And he went on about this particular product, and the benefits of
the package. But the main emphasis was on their money not being
at risk, because the company's outcome was that the clients didn't
lose all of their money. That was the first presentation.

Then someone from the rival company came on stage, and said:

> "When we designed this particular product we wanted to make
> sure that our clients got a really *good return* on their money. Now
> we can't say that our product is *totally safe*. No investment is
> totally safe. But we will ensure that you *get a return* on your
> money, even though we can't *guarantee its safety*."

After the presentations each speaker retired to their own booth,
where prospective clients could come up and talk to them. Out of
the 45 people at this presentation, only five of them went to the
first company, while the other 40 were queuing up at the second
one. The message put across in each case was essentially the same,
but the internal representations that the audience created were
very different.

So whenever you are presenting or training, when you say something to someone:

● *Say it the way you want it.*

This is a really important point: Leave them with what you want
them to think about, rather than what you *don't* want them to
think about. For example, you could screw up in sales by saying:
"I don't want you to think that our product is too expensive."
They might not have thought it before, but they will now.

At one company where we were doing some training, we were listening in on somebody selling over the phone. He started very
well, and we thought he was going to get the deal. Then for no
apparent reason, he said: "I don't want you to think I am being

pushy." Instantly he was cut off. He asked, "What happened? I thought I had the deal". So we said, "Just think about what happens in your mind when we tell you 'I don't want you to think I am being pushy'". The person on the other end of the phone didn't think he was being pushy – until he made the suggestion.

Think about the letters you write to prospective clients. How many sales letters do you get saying, "This is what we do. I am sure that your company will be interested in what we have to offer. Please don't hesitate to contact me." Well, there are many companies that we are still hesitating about. And again, many film and theatre reviews end up with, "Don't miss it." So we don't.

Of course, you can deliberately use negatives to great effect. For instance:

> "Now it wouldn't be right for us not to say that you won't get this instantly. And we wouldn't want to suggest that everything you learn in this book you will be able to do automatically. It wouldn't be OK for us to say that, because we don't know whether you will actually be able to excel in all the exercises. So don't bother to notice."

By using negatives, you are matching a very common aspect of our culture. So you can twist the meaning around by using negatives to say it the way you want it.

In general you need to check: Are you leaving the people with the internal representation that you want them to be left with? Do they have a model of the world in which more things are now possible?

Chapter Three
Your Internal State

Your State

We have already been considering how what we think affects our behaviour and our state – our physiology. My heart is beating normally again now.

The state you are in will affect everything else going on in you and around you. Therefore you need to know about states:

- how to be in the right state for what you want to do; and
- how to be able to change your state at will.

This chapter is about how the things going on inside our heads change our behaviour (*Figure 3.1*).

Figure 3.1

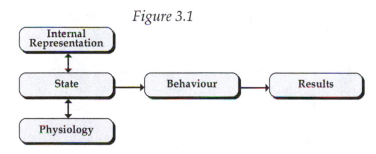

State means your emotional state, the way that you are feeling at any moment: You may be feeling happy or sad, feeling slightly depressed, or regretting not having studied NLP before. Perhaps you're feeling excited, highly energised, or very confident.

When you are feeling really good in yourself, you are probably going to behave differently than if you are not feeling good about yourself. You know this in your own experience. Compare your behaviour in those good times with the not-so-good times. A good state enables you to get far better results. So the middle line in *Figure 3.1* is saying:

- *To a large extent the way you feel inside determines the results you get.*

The *internal representation* on the top line in *Figure 3.1* is the same internal representation as we illustrated with the door and hinge in *Figure 2.1*. Here is a brief thought experiment for you to do:

> Now just for a moment, think about an event in the past, where you did something and it didn't work out the way you wanted it. And as you think about that event now, how do you feel?

Notice how you are feeling in your body as you think about that. You probably don't feel so good. OK. Come back to the present. Take a breath, and as you breathe out, let that memory go.

> Now think of a time when you did something in the past which worked out absolutely fantastically, and you did an even better job than you thought you would do.

Now, how do you feel? Do you notice that you feel different? Great.

So the next finding is that:

● *What you hold in your mind determines the way you feel.*

Your physiology
On the bottom line in *Figure 3.1* is *Physiology*. Imagine this scenario: we'll follow the fortunes of someone in sales, someone participating in a training such as *Presenting Magically:*

In their business life, this salesperson has a new deal on the table, a deal so lucrative that it offers the possibility of meeting all target goals for the year in one contract. As the salesperson arrives at the training, their mobile phone rings. It is the particular prospective client for the lucrative new deal, who says, "I'm sorry, but we have given the contract to your competitor".

Now, you would probably know that something like that had happened to that person before they told you. What would let you know? The evidence would be in their physiology – their 'body-language'. You would notice their posture: head down, walking relatively slowly, dragging their feet. Their facial expression could possibly be flat, definitely not smiling.

Now suppose that their mobile phone rings, and they go outside to answer it. It is the same prospective client. What has happened is that suddenly there has been a major change in the organisation, and the deal is back on. Except for one thing. The deal is now three times bigger than it was before.

Again, as the salesperson comes back in the room you would notice that something like that had happened because of the change in physiology. Now they are walking in a more animated fashion, their posture is more upright, their head is held high, and they are smiling.

So the next finding is:

● *The way you feel can change your physiology.*

The inverse is also true:

● *Your physiology can change the way you feel.*

These two are linked together. The way that you feel and your physiology are intimately connected. Change your physiology, and you will change the way you feel. Let's test this out. Actually do this, rather than just reading about it.

For this next piece you may want to have someone read the instructions to you in the manner indicated. Or you could record it onto tape yourself, and do the exercises when you play it back.

Exercise 2: Taking on Different States

Stand up. Now, just for a moment, get depressed. How would you be standing if you were depressed? Head down, looking at the floor. What would you be saying to yourself? "Oh, no! Why me? Why does this always happen to me . . . ?"

So get depressed for just a moment.

Yes, you're good at that. OK. Now just shake that off. Move your whole body, shake your arms and legs vigorously, and breathe again, so that none of that depressed stance remains.

Now stand with your feet about shoulder width apart, and begin to tense the muscles in your legs. Then tense the muscles in your calves, tense the muscles in your thighs. Now tense all the muscles in your hips, your stomach and your lower back. Now tense the muscles across your chest. Tense the muscles in your arms. Really, really tense. And the muscles all across your back. Now look up at the ceiling, roll your eyes up so that you are looking out of the top of your head. Put a massive grin on your face, so that you are showing your teeth. So that if someone were observing you from outside, they would think, "This must be a dental convention!" Big grin, loads of teeth, and say to yourself, inside your head, in an excited voice, "Yes, yes, yes, yes, yes, yes, yes, yes, yes, yes," just inside your head. *(speaking very quickly)*

Now, keeping everything exactly the same as it is right now, try and get depressed. Go on, try. You were good at this earlier. Try and get depressed, keeping everything exactly the same as it is now, try and get depressed. Come on, you know you were good at this. Can you do it?

No, you can't do it, can you? Exactly. OK, you can relax now.

You can't do depression standing and tensing all your muscles, looking up at the ceiling with a big grin on your face, saying, "Yes, yes, yes," to yourself, because your neurology doesn't work that way.

No more excuses
If you regularly work out at a gym, or go running, or engage in some kind of sport or dancing, then consider: How long does it take after a really bad day, for all the feelings of a bad day to disappear after you start exercising? A couple of minutes? It may take five minutes at the most. This is because the physiology of working out, or exercising energetically, is totally opposite to the physiology of a bad day.

So here is the deal on this:

● *You can change the way you feel – whenever you want.*

This means that the way you feel is under your control. It means that you can choose to be in the state that will get you the result you want.

Here is the downside to it:

● *There are no more excuses.*

If you are in the habit of arriving at your office saying, "Well, I don't feel so good today, because I fell out with my husband/wife/boyfriend/girlfriend/person I live with . . . before I left this morning," you now know that this won't work any more. Change your state, look up at the ceiling, put a big grin on your face and say, "Yes, yes, yes, yes, yes!" That will change your state, and it will change the state of everyone else in the office as well.

No matter what has happened to you, no matter what state you are in, you can change it so that you can get the result you want. That puts your results under your control in every area of your life. For example, you can enable your students to learn more easily, whether they are adults, college students, or children at school. In a sales presentation it will enable you to get more sales. Things just work better when you are in the appropriate state.

You can change your state, because it is your state. You can change what you are thinking, what is happening inside your head, what you are concentrating on. You can also change your physiology at will. Most of the people we meet during our trainings are in control of their physiology. That might not be true after closing time on a Saturday night, but generally, we assume that people have control over their physiology. You can use this fact to your advantage.

When we first discovered this concept, we thought it meant that everyone needed to be in an energised state all the time. However, it is appropriate to sleep every now and again! You need to have sufficient sleep, and that will certainly make it much easier for you to be in the appropriate state for presenting and training. Since you will be using energy while you are presenting or training, you must have enough in reserve. Think of it as having some sort of 'energy bank account'. Only when you have sufficient energy resources will you be able to do your stuff. If you over-draw your account, you will feel tired, exhausted, and otherwise less than exquisite.

In Chapter Ten you will learn some simple exercises that will allow you to increase the amount of energy you have. Doing these exercises on a daily basis, or just before you do a training, will ensure that you have more energy than you will ever need to take you all the way through the presentation, or through the day. Just imagine that you are putting an energy deposit into your account, which then becomes a resource you can draw on whenever you need to.

Getting into role . . .
David recalls: I once came across a sales guy who had a particular method of getting himself into the right state. If he arrived at a client's site and he wasn't in an empowered state, we would get out of the car, and with a rolled-up newspaper that he always car-ried with him, he would, start beating his car. He would thrash the back of his car, rather like that scene in *Fawlty Towers* when Basil Fawlty lashes his broken-down car with a branch. This sales guy would get into a really energised state from beating his car, so that when he walks into his sales presentation, he is emanating, "Hi! I'm here!" And people think, "Wow! Who's this just walked in through the door!?" This man changes his state because he knows there is no point in going to the meeting if he isn't in the right state. In other words:

● *Only by being in the right state will you get the result you want.*

You have to decide which state is going to enable you to get the result that you want:

● *What would be the appropriate state for the result you want, for your outcome?*

Having an outcome in mind will tend to take you into that state.

Who am I?

You may be asking: Is it not true that if you are changing your state all the time, if you are feeling bad, and you talk yourself into feeling good, then you're not really being yourself? The truth is that you are always in some state. When you change your state, you're still you. Because you are more than just the way you feel. You are much more than the way you are feeling right now. If you were only the person you are when you are feeling bad, then you would always feel bad. But you don't, because sometimes you feel good. You are always more than the way you feel at any particular time, and you will still be you, however you feel.

If, when you have your desired result, you want to go back to feeling bad, feel free. But if you have just done a brilliant presentation or training, you will probably want to stay feeling good. Remember:

- *You can choose how you feel, and you can change your state whenever you like.*
- *When you are doing some particular activity, the state you are in will determine your success at it.*

Chapter Four
Your Unconscious Mind

Let us introduce you to a very important part of yourself – your unconscious mind. Just go inside and say "Hello" to your unconscious mind. And notice what happens. Do you get a response? You know you have an unconscious mind, but you may not have been formally introduced before.

One way of thinking of your unconscious mind is that it is everything you are not consciously thinking of right now. As soon as you think of something, it becomes conscious. Before that it was in your unconscious mind. A quick demonstration:

Everyone has a conscious and an unconscious mind, so whenever you are with someone, you can communicate with both their conscious and unconscious minds, because we know that both parts are listening.

Figure 4.1

Figure 4.1 summarises what your unconscious mind does for you. The first thing to appreciate is that your unconscious mind is the source of all learning, all behaviour and all change. Here are some reasons why it is important for you to get to know your unconscious mind, and to consciously decide to communicate with other people's unconscious minds. We'll examine each of these individually:

Learning

Learning is not the domain of your conscious mind. Your unconscious mind is the part of you that learns. Now, you may have thought that you learned consciously in the past, and although learning must first go through the conscious mind, it is your unconscious mind that remembers everything. Everything, once learned, resides in the unconscious mind.

Think about all the things you have ever learned. Until the subject was mentioned, how many of them did you remember consciously? Probably none!

Think of all the phone numbers you have learned, and which you now know. For example, you know your home phone number, do you not? If you'd like to do this with us, please say it to yourself. Now before you were thinking of your home phone number, where was it? Obviously it was stored somewhere, a place of which you were not conscious – that is your unconscious mind – the part of your mind of which you are not conscious, right now. What's important about that is that all your learning – everything you have ever learned – is stored in your unconscious mind.

Behaviour

Students in the hypnosis seminars we teach often approach us and ask, "Can you make me move my arm unconsciously?" We ask the student if s/he had ever considered that s/he cannot move his/her hand consciously. Do you know how many muscles there are between the tip of your fingers and your shoulder blade? There are 159 muscles. So, it is impossible to move your hand *consciously*. You have to move it *unconsciously*. It's not just your hand, either – all behaviour is generated at the unconscious level. Think about walking. You just put one foot in front of the other, don't you? When you do, however, you don't think about it. You just do it. In fact if you think about walking, that thinking can be counter-productive. Thinking about walking is conscious thinking. The fact that it interferes with walking shows us that the behaviour is generated unconsciously.

How about this: The last time you drove to work, how conscious of it were you? Do you remember the whole trip? Or do you remember none of it? If you want a real scare, the next time you drive somewhere, just look over at the person next to you on the freeway. They too are probably unconscious.

Change
Think of a bad habit you wanted to change in the past. Was it easy? Probably not. Most people find it hard to change a bad habit. For them it's something that takes time. Tad remembers, "When my sideburns were long, I used to play with them all the time. One day I said, 'I'm not going to do that any more!' But, you know, five minutes later there I was again, playing with them".

If change was 'that' easy, you could walk up to a friend who was being a bit of a jerk and say, "Um, excuse me, but you're being a bit of a jerk! Would you please change?" And they would change. Right then – if change was conscious! In the real world, change isn't always that easy. Many people go on doing the same old things over and over, year after year, and they complain about it. If change isn't that easy for us, it is simply because we aren't fully in rapport with our unconscious mind. In the real world people are often not in rapport with the unconscious mind, and that is why change is sometimes difficult to accomplish.

So, all learning, behaviour, and change are unconscious. This makes the following idea vital to presenters.

Use positive language
Your unconscious mind cannot directly process a negative in consciousness. It's true. In fact, it's also true for the conscious mind. Think about this: You cannot think about what you wish to not think about without thinking about it. Think about that. For example, if we said, "Don't think about a blue tree," what are you thinking about? Unless you were semantically trained, you are probably thinking about a blue tree. Even though you were asked not to do that!!

Most of us go through our lives telling ourselves, "I don't want to think about a blue tree." When you go in to see the boss, do you say, "I hope he doesn't get angry like the last time"? When starting out in a new relationship, do you say, "Gee, I hope I don't get hurt"? Another example is the salesperson going in to make a sale and saying, "I hope I don't blow this sale."

If you or someone you know does that, it may be the wrong signal to be giving to the unconscious mind. It is the wrong signal because the unconscious mind cannot process a negative in consciousness. So, to facilitate communication between the conscious and the unconscious minds use positive, supportive language.

Chapter Five
Empowering Beliefs

In this chapter, you will explore how to become more flexible in your thinking by learning how people who are models of excellence tend to think – the assumptions they make about how the world works. These assumptions are known as the *Presuppositions* in NLP. They are common beliefs to people who are master communicators, whether they are teachers, therapists, presenters or trainers. To achieve comparable results, you must assume those beliefs for yourself, and operate in a similar model of the world.

Empowering Beliefs of Master Communicators

- Everyone has their own unique model of the world.
- In order to have rapport with another person, it is essential to respect their model of the world.
- The meaning of the communication is the response you get.
- There is no failure, only feedback.
- Resistance in an audience is a sign of lack of rapport.
- There are no resistant audiences, only inflexible presenters.

There is a saying, "Whether you believe you can or you can't, you are absolutely right". These NLP presuppositions will work for you when you act as if they are true. Try these beliefs out in your own life and notice the results you get.

- *Everyone has their own unique model of the world*

In Chapter Two we looked at how people create their model of the world. Your own internal representation of your reality is unique. This is because you experience the world you live in according to the filters and preferences you have when paying attention to what is around you. Even identical twins have unique experiences, and thus different models of the world. This would also be true if you were cloned; you and your clone would each have a unique internal representation of reality.

Think about this in terms of the number of different internal representations, different models of the world, that you encounter when you are presenting to a group. Each person in the group has a unique model. So if you were assuming that everyone's model of the world is pretty much the same as yours ... Well, think again, because it isn't. Their models may be vastly different from yours. David once said to a group he was training, "I spoke with my mother this morning just after she had had an accident". He then asked the group what they were thinking of. "She'd had a car crash", said one. "She'd fallen downstairs", said another. Actually, she had knocked over her cup of coffee as she reached for the phone! The more we do NLP, the more we realise how utterly different people are. NLP provides numerous ways of describing these differences, and as you learn more NLP you will learn to make many significant discriminations. By doing that, you will then be able to match other people in their *model* of the world. We will be exploring some of these differences in Chapter Eleven on sensory preferences, and in Chapter Fourteen in terms of learning styles.

● *In order to have rapport with another person it is essential to respect their model of the world.*

To have rapport with another person, and communicate effectively with them, you need to respect their model of the world, no matter how different it is from yours, whether you 'approve' of it or not. If you are presenting to a group of people, all of whom have different models of the world, at variance with yours, you still need to respect all of them. This doesn't mean they are 'right' and you are 'wrong', or vice versa. If you assume that everyone is right – from their point of view – then these are just different models of the world. If you always assume that for everyone in the room, their model of the world is perfect for who they are, then you will always be able to effectively communicate with them.

● *The meaning of the communication is the response you get.*

Most people assume that they control the meaning of what they are communicating. Should someone else misunderstand them, it is that other person's fault. In the example above, David's mother knew what she meant. The way you understood the statement, the meaning you made of it, was probably different. So who is right?

The only way of knowing what the other person thought you meant, is from their response. How many times have you had an experience where you say something and someone responds in a completely unexpected way? For instance:

"Why have you got that stretcher?"
"You said your mother had had an accident."
"But I didn't say she needed a stretcher."
"That's what I thought you meant."
"No, I didn't mean that. We need just a cloth . . . "

So the meaning of your communication is the response you get. It doesn't matter what you thought you communicated, it doesn't matter what you meant to say. What matters is: *What meaning did the other person get?*

If it is not what you intended, then it is up to you, as the master communicator, to be flexible and find other ways of getting your message across, until they do get it.

Consider the responses you get as information about how successfully you have communicated your message. Even no response is a still a response; whatever happens is information, because you cannot not communicate. The audience provides you with clues about what you may choose to do next, which ties in with the next presupposition.

● *There is no failure, only feedback.*

All responses from other people are simply feedback. Having this belief means you will always be able to get the response you want, because if you don't get it the first time, all you have to do is go on doing different things until you do get the response you want.

Quite often we think that if we do one particular behaviour and it doesn't work, then by doing it again and putting more effort into it, it will work the next time. If someone doesn't understand what you're saying, you repeat it, only LOUDER, or more s-l-o-w-l-y.

We assume that by saying the same words again the listener will understand it. What we suggest is that if you don't get the result you wanted, do anything other than what you just did, because you have just found one way that doesn't work. Now that doesn't mean you have failed. All it means is that you got some feedback. So heed the feedback, and do something different next time.

● *Resistance in an audience is a sign of lack of rapport.*

If you interpret the response you are getting from an audience as meaning 'They are resistant', then all that means is that you haven't got enough rapport with them yet. Since the responsibility for building rapport is yours, build more rapport. Once you have a good level of rapport, you will find that the audience 'resistance' disappears, or melts away. You could say:

● *There are no resistant audiences, only inflexible presenters.*

If you have ever been with a group, and started thinking, "They are a resistant audience", then that was less about a particular quality of the audience, and much more about your rigidity as a presenter! This is another example of your beliefs filtering your experience. As a presenter it is far more useful to acknowledge that you haven't yet found the best way to present or communicate with this particular group to get the result you want.

As an excellent presenter you will notice the responses you are getting from your audience and know whether or not you are on track for the results you want. If you're not, you need to change what you are doing, find a way of communicating differently, while still maintaining rapport, so that the next time you do get the results you want the next time.

Increasing your flexibility
So how do you increase your flexibility? 'Simply doing something different' may seem rather vague, too open-ended. First of all, acknowledge that you need to start at your end of the communication loop. This is where you can begin to make changes, because you have direct access to your own thinking and behaviour. This

is where your power lies. Wanting to change other people, to make them more flexible is much harder, so start with yourself.

Every time you assume that things go wrong or don't work by blaming other people, or fate, or any external 'cause', you are shifting responsibility away from yourself, which makes changing much harder. By blaming particular people, or the universe in general, you are giving away your power. If you continue to do that, there is no way that any training will ever go well, because you are no longer in a position of power.

The power to make changes lies within you. When you realise that you are actually the creator of everything that happens, you will be acting as a role model for others. Then your audience will also start being responsible for their own changing. Again, this is a useful belief to have. We don't know if it is true, but if you think this way, you will always be able to do something to get what you want. As soon as you go into blaming mode, with, "It's their fault . . ." then you might as well leave, because there is no way you are going to get your outcome.

Results or Reasons

Thinking about this in a business context. You ask someone to do something for you, and they don't do it. When you query them, they give you their reasons for not doing it.

- In business you always get one of two things: *results* or *reasons*.

You either get the result you want, or you get reasons, but actually, they aren't really reasons.

- There are no reasons: there are only *excuses*.

We use excuses that prevent us getting the result we want. There are only two options: you either get the result, or you have an excuse.

Here is a typical exchange we experience in our trainings:

> "I don't have excuses."
> "Oh, really. Do you get all the results you want?"
> "No."
> "So what do you get instead?"
> "I have good reasons."
> *"Whoa! There are no good reasons. That's just another way of saying excuses."*

Your favourite excuses
So here we are back in the world of negatives again. Remember that concentrating on your excuses, the negatives, you are reinforcing the things you don't want. And your favourite excuses will be ensuring that you don't get the results you want. Therefore, whenever you find yourself coming up with an excuse, turn it around, and restate things in terms of what you want instead. Say it the way you want it.

Think about the excuses people often use for sales presentations.

> "They probably aren't ready for us."
> "I think we are probably a little bit ahead of the field. I don't think they are quite on our wavelength yet. So that is why we didn't get the deal."

Or for mediocre trainings:

> "I think the reason some people in the training didn't get the result they wanted was because they were slow learners."

As soon as you engage in that kind of verbal mystification, there is no way you can get the result. Turn the excuses around, and take responsibility:

● I need to be more flexible.
● I need to respect other people's models of the world, so that I can match them.

In other words, we are back at the presuppositions of master communicators. The people who do get results have those presuppositions in place, go out there with the result they want in mind, and with the attitude of curiosity and wanton experimentation, they keep going until they get it. Whenever they find themselves coming up with an excuse, they tell themselves "That is not helping me get what I want. I need to do something different".

Dying to be right

Whatever you believe, you always get to be right. You either have an excuse, or you get the result you want. When we worked with many company managers, teaching them about NLP, presentations, rapport, and so on, together we have transformed the results in their company. On the other hand, we have worked with some company owners who have said, "I don't think it will work here". They were right. And they went out of business. Some people are willing to go out of business in order to be right. And because we work with people on health issues as well, we have even known people die to be right.

Every time you act as though these NLP presuppositions are true, you will make them true. That action will transform your stage presence, whether you are presenting or training, or at a business meeting.

* * * * * * * * * * * * * * *

One essential thing about getting what you want, is noticing if you are actually getting it. Sometimes when you ask people what they want, especially in a business environment, they say they want things they already have, but just hadn't noticed! So it is essential to pay attention to the feedback you are getting, to notice if you are on track.

Conversely, you will also be providing feedback for others about how they are doing. Giving feedback is an art, and we are going to examine that in the next chapter.

Chapter Six
Feedback

By feedback, we mean more than some ticked boxes on the 'happiness sheet' that you collect from your group at the end of the course. The NLP communication model suggests that all the information available through your senses is potentially feedback to you. You are constantly getting feedback, although you will be filtering that information for what you consider relevant at that particular time. Whenever you are presenting or training, feedback from the group allows you to monitor how they are at any time during the presentation or training – if you pay attention to it.

'Feedback' is also used in a more limited sense to mean consciously giving someone specific information about how they are doing at a given activity. Since you are often going to be offering considered feedback to the people you are teaching, training or coaching, we want you to know how to do it effectively.

The feedback sandwich
This particular feedback model enables people to easily change their behaviour. It comes from a research study done by an NLP colleague – Master Trainer Wyatt Woodsmall. He did some work for the US Army to teach officers how to give their new recruits effective feedback. Perhaps they had found that the screaming-in-the-ear technique didn't work! Their brief was: 'How do we give feedback to people so that it works?'

This is what they found.

Give people feedback within five minutes
For feedback to be effective, you have to give it within five minutes of occurrence of the specific behaviour. Although the conscious mind can handle delay, feedback works more powerfully with the unconscious mind. Because much can happen in

five minutes, make the connection as soon as possible, while the link to the behaviour is still intact.

Tell them what they did well.

You give feedback only on the things they did well: "You did this well, you did that well . . . " Be really specific on the behaviours they did that worked.

Then tell them what they could do even better next time, or what they could do differently next time that would make it even better.

It is extremely important that this time, you make no reference to what they did that *didn't* work. When you give feedback, focus on only the positive: what they could do that would enable them to get an even better result.

This is not just the power of thinking positively, that everything is wonderful. Remember 'Don't think of a blue tree'. If you say to someone "You did *x* and it didn't work", they are now thinking about what you don't want them to do any more, and the fact that it didn't work. That is reinforcing what doesn't work.

Give them an overall positive comment

Overall positive comments would be:

"That was a really good presentation."
"I was entertained by what you were doing."
"You're really good at this."

Some other useful findings, for coaching, training, or managing other people, that came from this study are:

If you actually tell someone that they did something well, they will do more of it.

So if you say "You did this, and it was really good", they will do it again.

We have also found over the years that if you tell someone that they are good at something that they either didn't do or they weren't good at, in all probability they will be better at it next time.

So if someone didn't do a particular behaviour, and you say "You did this, and it was absolutely brilliant!" the chances are they will be brilliant at it when they do do it.

Giving the Feedback

If you want someone to improve, consider the following: They will hear more of what you have to say and be more willing to accept your communication, if you have rapport with them. Having rapport means they will be feeling safe and comfortable with you. And because you are giving them all positive feedback, they are far more likely to take it in, and change how they are thinking about themselves and what they do. (We will cover rapport in detail in Chapter Eight.)

This might be a different feedback model from any you have previously experienced, either when receiving feedback from someone, or when giving it to others. If you are used to receiving feedback like "You did this wrong. You did that all wrong. That was terrible. And you didn't do a very good job with that either", then this is the total opposite. It may seem strange, or even naive at first, but we know this works, because we have been using it in all of our trainings since we began. If you are used to giving feedback another way, then we suggest you suspend judgment on this, and try it out. Act as if what we are telling you is true, give feedback this way, and notice the difference in the results you get.

Whatever it takes
Some people's first response to this way of giving feedback is that somehow it is not genuine or honest. But when you experience feedback in this way, you will find it to be very honest and very direct, given to you in an empowering way that will enable you to do things differently next time, rather than tell you what you didn't do well last time. The purpose or intention of the feedback, is to enable you to get the result of being a magnificent presenter

and trainer. Our intent is to do whatever it takes to enable people to attain that outcome.

You might be wanting to give someone feedback and thinking, "Hmm, I'm not sure. Am I just saying they did that really well, but not really believing it?" Or maybe you think someone is really bad at something, and wonder how you can then give positive feedback to them. Actually you can always find things that they do well, even if you have to make them up. And you can always find things to improve. By focusing on the positives you will find that they do indeed start improving.

One thing we ardently believe is that anyone can do anything that they want to. They might not be demonstrating it at the moment, but if they really want to do it, then we believe that they can – no matter what it is, no matter where they start from, or where it is they want to go. Because if we didn't think that, then we shouldn't be working with them. If we were to think, "This person isn't going to be able to do this", then that belief could be preventing them from doing it.

So when we are working with someone in a group or on a one-to-one basis, we have the belief that they can get the result they want, provided they are willing to do whatever it takes to get it. We know that we are prepared to do whatever it takes to enable someone to get the result – then they will get the result.

Think about this in relation to your own outcomes, what you want from reading this book. Wherever you are right now:

● Are you willing to do whatever it takes to get the result you want?

Because if you are, provided you have an outcome in mind, and you are willing to do whatever it takes, you will get there.

Reaping the Benefits

After trainings students have told us, "I was amazed at how much I achieved during the training, and I've really changed as far as presentations are concerned. I didn't think I would remember it all, but when I got in front of an audience, about three hundred people . . . " – which they weren't used to. They came to the training because this event was looming in their future – " . . . I went on stage, and instantly forgot everything I was meant to be doing . . . and I did it all, automatically."

One student was a hypnotherapist who had not done any presentations before. He worked for the police force and was a hypnotherapist part-time. One day the police superintendent asked him to do a evening talk on hypnotherapy, because he thought it would be useful for stress control within the police force. The money people were paying to attend would be going to charity. So he said:

"OK, I'll do it. So how many people normally turn up?"
"About twenty-five."
"I think I can handle that."

When he turned up on the evening, there were 200 people in the audience! Backstage he was thinking about the decision he'd made . . . But then he realised, "This stuff I learned. It doesn't matter whether I am with one person or two hundred. As long as I do what I've learned, I'll be OK". So he came out on stage, saw these two hundred faces in front of him, and the first thing he did was to go into the trainer state. (You will be doing this in the next chapter.) By standing there and going into the trainer state, all of his nervousness and all his fear completely disappeared.

He told us, "And then I did the whole two-hour presentation on autopilot. And I received standing ovation. But when I came off stage I couldn't remember what I'd done". Have you ever had a standing ovation from two hundred people? It is quite a powerful experience!

* * * * * * * * * * * * * * *

49

In these opening chapters we have been setting some frames, giving you some theory and explaining how NLP can be applied to this way of presenting. Now that we have this in place, we are ready to start doing some exercises, and you will be doing these throughout the rest of the book. Essentially, we will be teaching you how to be comfortable being yourself in front of any audience. You'll have to put something in, too, because you have to learn it. We can't learn it for you. So when you do the exercises, do them to the best of your ability. Even if you are thinking that you can't remember everything you have covered so far, or that not all of it makes sense yet, then we suggest that you trust your unconscious mind. When you do that in the exercises, you will find that what you need will be there, and this will totally transform the way you present, to such an extent that you will look back in amazement at that earlier version of you who did any previous presentations before you read this book.

The rest of this book is very practical. It gives you the how-to's. And the most important how-to is establishing and maintaining rapport with your audience. With rapport, everything becomes much easier, much more effective. You will learn how to do that, both on a one-to-one basis, and also with groups, but only after we have explored what you need to pay attention to in yourself – your state.

Chapter Seven
States for Learning and Training

We looked at states in Chapter Three. Now, you are going to learn two states that are particularly relevant in the learning process, the learning state and the trainer state. The learning state is the one to be in when you are on the receiving end of someone else's training, or when you are doing private study. The trainer state is vitally important whenever you are presenting or training.

The Learning State

You are learning all the time by engaging with the world, attending live trainings, or interacting with books, videos, or CD-ROMs. All learning is processed by the unconscious mind, which is filtering and sorting all our experiences as well as storing our memories. The conscious mind is not designed to work in that way. As we stated earlier, it would be overloaded by the vast amount of information arriving incessantly.

Memories are accessed, based on the state you are in when you were learning. That state is also coded as part of the memory. Therefore to retrieve that information, you need to be in that same state again. Some memories are accessible *only* when you are in that state. So if you are having difficulties remembering something, it could mean you need to first match that state. Then you will find the information you want is readily accessible.

The best state for learning is a light trance state. You will be able to retrieve the information most easily if you go into that light trance state again. Here's how to go into a light trance.

It may be easier to have someone read you the instructions, or you make a tape recording to play back. When reading the instructions, speak softly and slowly, in a trance-like manner. In other words, be in the state you want other people to go into by going into it slightly yourself.

For this exercise you need to have something to look at comfortably across the room, above eye level. This could be a small object, mark, or picture on the wall, or you could make a black or coloured spot out of paper, and stick in on the wall about four feet above head height. It may also be useful to have some slow, 'trancy' music playing in the background. We use music a lot in training, as it is a good way of inducing certain states – as you will know from listening to movie soundtracks.

Exercise 3: The Learner State

Here are the words to use for this process *(Read this slowly, with plenty of pauses)*:

First of all, relax, get comfortable, preferably sitting down with both feet on the floor.

Fixate your attention by focusing on the spot up on the wall. All you have to do is look at the spot. Just put your eyes up and look at that spot, simply focus in on the spot.

And as you focus on the spot for a moment, while still looking at the spot, begin to expand your awareness. Let your awareness flow out into the periphery, into the space round the spot. You are putting your awareness into peripheral vision. So as you keep looking at the spot, you may notice, even as you are looking at the spot, that you can see other things around in the room. While looking at the spot, you can see the walls, and the ceiling, and some of the other things in the room in peripheral vision, even though you are focusing on the spot. And continue to open up your awareness into the periphery. So even though you are looking at the spot, you can become aware in your periphery of any people on either side of you, and the furniture, the walls on either side.

Then pull your awareness around even further . . . so that you are also aware of what is happening behind you, even though you are still looking at the spot.

Now obviously you won't be able to see what is happening behind you, but you can become aware of what is happening behind you, or have the kind of sensations that you would have if you were able to see what is happening behind you.

So pull your awareness all the way round, pull it all the way around behind you, so even though you are looking at the spot, you are aware of what is behind you, and you are allowing your peripheral vision to reach into the corners of the room behind you.

(You may find this easier to do by imagining there is a ball just above and behind the back of your head. And while you are still looking at the spot, put your attention or your awareness on that imaginary ball, above and behind the top of your head, and you will find that it will open up your awareness.)

Now keeping your attention in the periphery, still keeping your awareness on what is happening around you, bring your eyes down, so that your eyes are looking straight ahead . . . keeping your awareness in the periphery. So you can see what is straight in front of you, and yet your awareness is all the way around the outside, your attention is now in the entire room.

(If you had some music playing, now is the time to slowly fade the music . . .)

And notice this state that you are in. This state might seem a little bit weird at first, a little bit spacey . . . That's OK. So just staying in that state . . . while you are in that state, how do you notice you feel differently now?

Do this exercise now.

Debrief

People report that they feel larger, more open, more space inside; that they are present and not present at the same time; that they are aware of a lot more, but don't see anything very clearly. All of these feelings are OK. When you go into peripheral vision, you slightly defocus your eyes from what you are looking at in the centre of your field of vision. The resulting feeling of being more open and relaxed means that you are in a light trance, which is a good state for learning.

When we taught children how to do this, their grades increased between one and two points, like from B to B plus, or B to A minus or A, over the space of a term. They learn to go into this state when they are in class. And then when they do an exam or test they are able to go into the same state again, and remember what they have done.

So whenever you are in a classroom, lecture hall, or auditorium, if you go into this state, you will find it easier to learn the material you are presented with, and you will be better able to remember all the information. You will also be nicely relaxed, and more open to what is happening.

The Trainer State

The trainer state, or presenter state, is essential for what you are going to be doing. This is the state you go into at the start of a presentation or training, when you first stand in front of the audience. As you enter the trainer state, you become relaxed, open, aware of everything going on around you, and able to respond to what is happening in the room.

Figure 7.1 The trainer state

Adapted from Patanjali's *Yoga Sutras* – 600 AD

1. **Yama**	}	Taking care so that there is nothing else going on in your life
2. **Niyama**		
3. **Asanam**		Get physiologically stable and comfortable, seated if you wish
4. **Pranayam**		Control your breathing – calm the breathing
5. **Pratyahara**		Withdraw your attention momentarily – turn it inside
6. **Dharana**		One-pointed attention – pick a point of focus
7. **Dhyana**		Allow the awareness to expand
8. **Samadhi**		Become one (with the room)

The eight steps in *Figure 7.1* have been adapted from 1400-year-old writings called Patanjali's *Yoga Sutras*. The words on the left are transliterations of the original Sanskrit. On the right are some brief interpretations, which have been interpreted in the context of presenting or training. Let us examine each step:

1. **& 2.** As soon as you stand in front of an audience, no matter what else is going on, no matter what has happened beforehand, when you do *Yama* and *Niyama*, put all of it out of your mind. The only thing you are thinking about is what you are doing right here and now, with this audience.

3. *Asanam* means get physiologically comfortable. Although you may think you are physiologically comfortable slumped in front of the television, or sprawled on the beach, that is not what it means here. The following short process will

teach you know to how to be physiologically comfortable and balanced when you are presenting.

Stand with your body's centre of gravity over your heels, balanced, upright and symmetrical. You may find this easier by imagining you are standing with each foot on a set of bathroom scales. When you are balanced, both scales will read the same weight – half of your body weight. If you are unbalanced, one side will read more than the other.

Now imagine that your body is made up of several cylinders representing the bony parts of your body: skull, ribcage, pelvis, legs and arms. These cylinders are connected by flexible joints. Imagine you are a marionette puppet, supported from above by a string coming out of the crown of your head. When this string is pulled up, your spine lengthens, and all the other sections of your body will naturally align themselves so that you are, as it were, hanging loosely and symmetrically, and you will be balanced forward and back. Your arms will naturally fall straight down by your sides.

Any tension you have may manifest in your arms and hands, so that you cross your hands in front of you, the 'figleaf' position, or clasp your hands behind, in the 'Prince Charles', or 'reverse figleaf' position. Being physiologically comfortable means you will release this tension, and just let the arms and hands hang loose.

4. *Pranayam* is to get your breathing under control. Typically what happens for many people when they start their presentation is they take a deep breath . . . and hold it. This doesn't actually work very well for putting you in a good state for presenting. You do need to keep breathing. You can get your breathing under control by breathing in through your nose . . . and breathing out slowly through the mouth.

Do some of these breathing cycles now:

● Take a deep breath in through your nose

- Then breathe out slowly through your mouth
- Repeat.

Now breathe normally again. This will calm you down, as you begin to bring your breathing under your conscious control.

5. *Pratyahara* is to withdraw your attention momentarily from the audience and go inside, putting all of your attention inside yourself.

6. *Dharana* is to concentrate on one thing. So find a spot at the back of the room that you can look at comfortably, and focus all of your attention on that spot.

7. *Dhyana* is to contemplate or expand your awareness. Look at your spot, and expand your awareness, just as you did in Exercise 3. When you are in front of an audience, expand your awareness to take in all four corners of the room: the two in front of you and the two corners behind you. Even though you are looking at the spot, you are aware of everything happening in the room, including every movement the audience is making.

8. *Samadhi* is having the sense of being at one with the room. It is as though the separation or boundaries between you and the audience disappear. At that moment, you will be aware of everything that is happening both in you and everyone else, which means you are open to feedback that lets you know how things are going.

Exercise 4: How to get into the Trainer State

Assume that you are doing this in front of an audience. Stand in the position you would be in, and have someone read out these instructions, so that you can go into the trainer state:

Put any other concerns out of your mind, so that you are totally present and aware of what is happening right here and now.

Now get physiologically comfortable. You may need to move a little from foot to foot, a little bit to each side, or a little bit forward and backward, until you find that point where the scales would be reading the same weight . . . Allow yourself to extend slightly upward, so that you are totally aligned, hanging loose, physiologically comfortable, with your arms relaxed by your sides . . .

Get your breathing under control: so take a deep breath in through your nose . . . let it out through your mouth . . . and then just continue to breathe naturally.

And now go inside for a moment. Pull all of your attention inside, and focus your awareness inside yourself . . .

Now bring your awareness back outside, to the room, and focus on a spot on the back wall. Put all your attention there, concentrate on that spot. And, still looking at the spot, expand your awareness to fill the entire room, so that you are aware of everyone and everything in the room, even though you are looking at the spot . . .

Continue to expand your awareness and have your awareness roll into the far corners of the room . . . bring it all the way down the sides . . . pull it around behind you. While still focusing at the spot, your awareness is in all four corners of the room, and you are aware of everyone and everything in the room.

And notice that while you are in this state, every small movement that your audience is making seems to be very obvious or even exaggerated.

And as you do this, allow the feeling of being at one with all the people in front of you. And being at one, now bring your eyes down and look at the group.

Begin to experiment with making eye contact with certain people in the group, while remaining in peripheral vision. Even though you are looking at one particular person, your awareness is still in the entire room.

And notice how much more awareness you have of everything that is happening in the room . . . in peripheral vision . . . in this trainer state.

This trainer state is one of being totally present, calm and balanced inside, ready for anything. In other words, it enables you to present and train magnificently. If you arrived to do your presentation or training feeling nervous or fearful, by doing each step completely, you will enter the trainer state, and those feelings will disappear. In the trainer state you cannot feel any negative feelings. If you do feel them, you are not in it properly, so you need to do some more of the steps.

Some people experience the final step, becoming one with the room, as being no longer fully there, almost disappearing in a sense. That's OK. When we first started doing presentations and trainings we didn't do a particularly good job because we were missing certain skills. If in the trainer state your conscious mind 'disappears', you can no longer do that. Operating unconsciously allows you to get out of your own way, so that you can present magically.

'Leveler' physiology
Some people, when they stand up to present, prefer not to be perfectly balanced with their weight evenly on both feet. Changing how you are standing to this balanced way may feel uncomfortable at first, simply because it is unfamiliar. Part of learning is about increasing your flexibility and using different physiologies. Even though it might not be how you usually present, it is worth getting used to presenting from this balanced position because of the message it sends to your audience. We are constantly communicating with our physiology. You need to know what message you are sending non-verbally to your audience. If you are unbalanced, lopsided, angular, or slumped, this may be at variance with the words you are saying. (More about this in Chapter Thirteen.)

Figure 7.2

This balanced, symmetrical position is called the 'Leveler' physiology (*Figure 7.2*). It communicates strength and stability, a no-nonsense approach: "This is the way it is. These are the facts."

Standing in this balanced position, bring both hands, palm down, from chest height, down your midline, and move them slightly outward to each side. Finish at waist-height, as though you are resting your hands on solid rock.

Present yourself this way if you want to get your message across to an audience and have them assimilate it. You will learn more about this in Chapter Thirteen.

In your training, you will be doing many of the preliminary exercises in this book in silence, because you are getting into the best state for training or presenting, learning to be comfortable being yourself. From the audience's point of view, you are simply standing there for a moment or so doing nothing while inside, you are running through the steps and becoming totally present.

Getting control of the group

In any group of people in a presenting and training context, the group will unconsciously seek for someone to be in control. If you are the presenter or trainer we suggest it should be you. If it isn't you, it will be someone else, which means that you won't have control of your audience. Therefore, it is essential to take control right at the beginning of your presentation or training.

One very effective way of covertly getting control of the group, is to stand on stage and do nothing. We have 'wantonly' experimented with this, just to see what happens. We have been standing there doing nothing, just being in the trainer state. It may be less than a minute, but subjectively it seems like an eternity. Gradually the conversations in the room stop, and it goes quiet. Now you have control.

Silence creates a vacuum, and most people in the audience want to fill it. The whole room will go silent, and they will be waiting expectantly, because they think you are going to say something important. They fill the silence with their attention, and you'll have their maximum attention for the next thing you say. Therefore, if you want to make a major point and ensure that the whole audience gets it, then pause . . . until you see, in peripheral vision, that everyone is waiting on you. And then you deliver it.

At the beginning of the book we gave another example of getting control of a group when talking about setting time frames. You can say something like:

> "Let me give you the schedule for the training, and because they are not in your manual, you may want to write these times down."

The key words here are, "You may want to write these down". When you are about to give the timing, pick up a pen. People in the audience also pick up a pen. Write the times on the flipchart, and say "You may want to write this down", and they do. Covertly now, you have control of the group. Rapport is the result of two (or more) people doing the same thing. The fact that we are all writing the times down, starts building rapport in the group. (See Chapter Eight.)

This is also useful in sales presentations. If you are wanting your prospective client to make a decision on what you are offering, and all the way through your presentations you have been asking them to do things, and they have done them, then when you come to the close, you are already in control of the situation. They are then far more likely to go with what you say.

In trainings, you need to have control of the group, because when you send people off to do exercises, you want them to come back. Trainings go better when that happens! If you say "Fifteen minutes for an exercise," and everyone leaves . . .

The more times you ask people to do things and they comply, the more you will have control. You might get compliance with the first thing you ask them to do, or you might get it after the fiftieth thing you ask them to do. The thing is – because there is no failure, only feedback – you just keep doing something different until you get the result.

Chapter Eight
Rapport

The Dance of Rapport

Rapport occurs when you match other people's behaviour, thinking, or levels of energy. You are meeting them in their model of the world. Rapport happens naturally when people become aware of each other and start communicating. It is like a dance in which one person leads and the other follows. People who are in rapport have a cooperative and harmonious way of being together, a sense of being mutually acknowledged, and know it is OK to be who they are. Rapport is value-free; it's neither good nor bad, but just a description of a matching.

Rapport works best when it is out of conscious awareness and arises spontaneously. However, it is still a learnable skill, and it is possible for you to enhance your rapport with others. In this chapter we will be exploring some of the ways in which you can establish and maintain rapport with individuals and with groups of any size.

Rapport is a prerequisite for effective communication, so before doing anything with a group, you must establish rapport with them. You have to be flexible enough to be able to enter into someone else's reality to an extent. When you do this, they will feel acknowledged and be willing to engage with you.

Definitions of rapport
Let's look at some definitions:

Rapport is the process that allows you to communicate and bond with your audience's unconscious mind. Work on the unconscious level because it is the unconscious mind that looks after all learning, all behaviour, and all change.

When you have rapport with your audience, they will be in a state in which they will uncritically accept suggestions that you are offering to their unconscious mind. With rapport, people tend to be more open to you, less critical, have fewer objections, and be more likely to accept what you have to say.

When people are like each other, they like each other. Rapport works by matching on all levels. 'Like' has these two connected meanings. Think about the people you like the most. They are probably like you in some ways, and have similar preferences. Establishing rapport is about creating likeness. When you do that, people will like you, and you will build rapport.

The communication of meaning

Many studies of the relative importance of different parts of human communication, language, gestures, facial expression, and so on, were carried out in the 1960s and 1970s. Professor Ray Birdwhistle studied bodily communication, which he called Kinesics. A classic study by Professor Albert Mehrabian showed that in human communication, only 7% of the meaning was carried in the actual words we used. He found that 38% was in the way we said the words (*Figure 8.1*). You have probably heard the saying "It's not what you say, it is the way that you say it". That study showed that overall the major part of your communication lies not in the actual words, but in everything else you are doing: how you say them and all the *non-verbal* aspects.

Figure 8.1

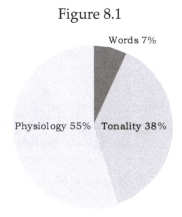

Words 7%

Physiology 55% Tonality 38%

When David was a child, his mother had one way of saying his name that made him feel really good, safe, and cared for. But sometimes she would say *"David . . ."* with a particular tonality, which would elicit a very different response in him: "Whoops, I think I had better go and hide." She had found him in the Christmas presents! The actual word was the same; how she said it conveyed very different meanings for him.

The remaining 55% of the communication has nothing to do with the words, or the way you say them. It has to do with your physiology: the way you hold your body, your posture, the way you stand, the way you sit, the way your breathe, the gestures you use, and the facial expressions you have. With your physiology, you provide a 'bodily' context for the other person to make sense of what you are saying.

So, if you are with other people, it is impossible to not communicate. Even if you are silent and motionless, you will still be communicating something. You might even be communicating more by being present and silent than you would by talking on the telephone – because the 55% of the communication from physiology is missing when you are on the phone.

Creating Rapport

You can build rapport with someone by matching their ways of communicating:

- Use the actual words they use. Use their jargon, their preferred terms, even if you think they are using the 'wrong' word. It is what it means to them that matters.
- Use the same tonality. Say the words the way they do.
- Adopt the same physiology. Use the same posture and gestures.

People create rapport, or a bond with others, by finding shared experiences. When you meet someone for the first time, you ask them questions to discover any common ground: perhaps you went to the same school, support the same football team, visited the same holiday location, like the same food, music, whatever. As soon as you find something in common, the relationship starts to form. Then the chances are you will begin adopting the same posture: you'll both have your arms folded, or one hand to your face, and so on. This will be happening out of conscious awareness. You are doing this all the time anyway, but may not have realised it until now.

Notice this in pubs and restaurants, wherever people are engaged in conversation or shared activity, how they tend to match or mirror each other. For example, people walking along the street will naturally fall into the same rhythm; in a pub, they will be leaning on the bar in the same way, raising their glasses simultaneously. When one person changes their physiology, their companion very soon follows. A couple sharing a meal in a restaurant will eat at the same time, drink at the same time. Should they begin arguing or disagreeing with each other, this rapport pattern will disappear, and they will have mismatching physiologies.

When you are in rapport with someone, and matching them in these ways, they will be paying attention to you, open to hearing what you have to say. You will probably have agreement – which could be useful. And because they like you, they will want to assist you in achieving your outcomes. So rapport smoothes the way for your being able to get the results you want.

Let's explore many of the ways you can match someone else to create rapport.

Matching physiology
Pay attention to someone's posture, gestures, and movement, and then match:

- The position of their head, shoulders, spine, arms, hands, torso, and legs.
- How they are sitting, standing, or walking – their gait.
- How they are sitting: legs crossed, or uncrossed?
- Weight distribution: is their spine upright, or curved with weight more to one side?
- Arm position: folded or open?
- Hand position: clasped, or open? Clenched or relaxed?
- The relationship between the head and the shoulders: is the head tilted to one side, or angled front to back?
- How much they move: are they still or in constant motion?
- Their facial expression: are they animated? Frowning or smiling? Animated eyebrows? Smiling? Showing their teeth?
- Any particular gestures?

Use the other person's gestures only when you are talking, not as they are talking, or you will draw attention to them, and they will wonder what you are doing. Rapport will then be lost.

- How they are breathing: deep or shallow? High up or in their belly?

Breathing
Breathing in sync with someone also occurs naturally. Getting rapport by matching breathing is easy on a one-to-one basis. This is how you do it.

- If someone is talking to you, they are breathing out. So when they are talking to you, you breathe out. When they pause for a breath, you breathe in.
- Notice, in peripheral vision, any rising and falling in the chest area. Don't stare! It's easier to see movement in the folds of their clothing. People get bigger as they inhale and smaller as they exhale, whatever their shape or sex. If you cannot detect movement in their chest area, watch their shoulders: they rise when they inhale, and fall when they exhale. It may be only a slight movement. You can see it easily from either the back or the front.

Exercise 5: Matching Physiology

Do this matching exercise with one other person. Take about three minutes each way.

This is what you do.

- One of you is A and the other B. The first part of this exercise is silent.
- A thinks of some past experience which has some emotional charge to it, some strong associated feelings, either positive or negative. A silently reruns the memory in their mind, like a movie, and gets the feelings back. That is all.
- B's job is to match A's physiology exactly: Sit in the same way, copy A's breathing, and breathe in sync with them. Match any facial expressions or gestures they use. If they

move around in their seat, do the same thing. Match every-thing. The only exception is, if A closes their eyes, you keep yours open. The exercise is much easier when you can see!

Once you have been matching for a couple of minutes:

- B tells A how they felt. Not what you think A is feeling, but how you actually felt while you were matching them. If any-thing came to mind in terms of what their event may be, tell them that as well.
- When you have done that, swap over and do it the other way.

Do both parts of this exercise with your partner now.

Debrief

People are often amazed when they do this, at how much accurate information they get about the other person's experience. Because your physiology is directly related to the state you're in, the feel-ings you're having, then if someone is experiencing a particular emotion, by adopting the same physiology as that person, you will experience the same feelings. Some people also have a good idea of what the event was, and the other person exclaims, "Wow! Are you psychic?" That is an indication of how much we commu-nicate with our physiology.

Once people have established rapport in an exercise, they will continue matching the other person's physiology while giving feedback or chatting after they have finished. This is good. They carry on exploring the relationship, and expand their conversa-tion. You as the trainer may even have a problem getting them back: "We're starting again!" and they are still chatting away.

This exercise may seem contrived, because it is making conscious that which normally happens unconsciously. But to learn how to do this, you need to be consciously aware of what you are doing. We all do this matching anyway, but we don't realise how it builds rapport. In this exercise, you consciously know, "This person is building rapport with me". In the future you will occasionally notice that you are matching people. Fine. Then you can go back to doing it unconsciously.

When first matching people, you might think it would be so obvious to them that they would ask, "Why are you doing the same thing as I am?" Having learned that anything to do with someone's physiology is completely out of conscious awareness, we decided to test it by copying people's physiology to a ridiculous extreme, all the time feeling uncomfortable, and thinking, "They must notice. They're bound to say something." But no one ever noticed. In general people aren't consciously aware of what they are doing with their own physiology, let alone what someone else is doing with theirs.

Relaying Rapport

An example of using matching happened when David was doing a training for a major organisation and he was introduced to the group by the marketing director. The director stood up and said a little bit about the training, and introduced David. As the director was talking he used some idiosyncratic gestures: his hands were out, palms forward, and he was rotating them side to side, as if he was waving at the audience. He had great control of the group, and great rapport with them. It was obvious they had a lot of respect for him.

When he finished, David went over and stood exactly where he had been standing, adopted the same physiology, and started giving the overview of the training. He used that same hand gestures, and instantly got the same response from the audience. Now since David had had many years of training experience, he got it straight away. Once he had rapport – and he could see that response in his peripheral vision – he went back to his stool and he started the training. But only after he knew he had all of the rapport, all of the attention, and all of the respect that the marketing director had got, and had transferred it all to himself.

Doing something like that accelerates your ability to quickly establish rapport with a group of strangers. The secret is to utilise everything that happens. 'Utilise' simply means that you accept what is happening, rather than trying to ignore or deny it. In any training or presentation there are going to be interruptions: people wandering in, noises off, things falling over, phones ringing. By simply accepting them – and often you will find that they will be weirdly appropriate to what you are doing at the time – making a quick comment, you can move on, which will be far better than trying to fight against the intrusion. When you are also in rapport with your environment in this way, then it is no big deal.

Everything you do creates a result. By increasing your awareness you are learning to *calibrate* to the results you are creating: the states you are eliciting, the behaviours you are triggering, the responses you are getting. By calibrating to your results, you can then do more of what works on purpose, so that you can get the results you want more efficiently.

Exercise 6: Matching and Agreement

The next exercise is about matching and agreement with your partner.

This is what you do:

- Find a subject on which you both agree.
- Talk about the subject on which you agree, while mismatching physiology.
- Do that for a couple of minutes, and notice what happens.
- Then find a subject on which you disagree.
- Discuss this topic on which you disagree while maintaining rapport and matching physiology, and notice what happens.

That's it. Common topics that people disagree on are things such as: politics, religion, euthanasia, nuclear armaments, animal experiments, and so on.

Do both parts of this exercise now.

Debrief

People often find this tricky, because they are working against a habitual pattern. When you are agreeing and mismatching, it is a challenge to keep mismatching, because the natural tendency is to match.

In general, if there is something that you disagree on, and you are still matching physiology, then the relationship continues. Remember the pie chart in Figure 7. The actual content is the least significant part of the communication. What matters is what you are doing with your body. Even though you are probably not consciously aware of what you are doing with your physiology, you are maintaining the rapport on a physiological level. Whether you are agreeing or disagreeing verbally is of minor importance. The relationship holds.

Therefore, when you are with someone with whom you possibly disagree, it is far more important that you match them with your physiology. You are still sending the message that you are with them, even though what you are saying may be at odds. Generally speaking, people maintain relationships more through rapport than by agreeing with everything they say to each other!

When you were doing the exercise, did you notice that when you were in rapport, you started appreciating the other person's point of view? Even if it was something you really didn't agree with before, you found that you could understand their position. This is a good position for reaching agreement.

If you are negotiating with someone, you may know there are certain items on which you strongly disagree. They may choose to continue to disagree with you, but if you spend time building rapport you will be able to keep the communication channels open. Then you can explore principles you have in common. It is always possible to reach agreement if you go to a high enough level of principle. For example:

- To make sure all parties are treated fairly.
- To increase profits for the business.

● To make the world a better place.
● To become more of who you really are.

You can probably get their agreement in principle. All that remains then is to find specific ways of satisfying that principle. You start checking the details in the light of the principle involved: 'Are these specific actions and conditions still in agreement with the general principle?' By cooperating in this way, maintaining rapport through matching on the level of principle, you will be able successfully to find solutions that satisfy everyone.

Breaking Rapport

You don't want to have rapport all the time. There are definitely times when you want to break rapport – for example, when you have to go to another appointment, to get on with your work, or simply to get away from someone who is taking up too much of your time! If it is time to leave them, start mismatching the other person to whatever degree is necessary. They will usually pick that up, and 'get the message'. And if they don't . . . simply say, using the Leveler physiology, "I have to go now". Subtly push both hands to one side, and walk away. This is a good reason for holding meetings in the other person's office; it is easier for you to choose when to leave!

In sales it is a good idea to break rapport just before the other person signs a binding contract. Momentarily break rapport so that they are committed to the contract, rather than to you, the sales person. You can say, "I just have to make a phone call", or find an excuse to leave the room so that they are signing it on their own.

At other times you may break rapport inadvertently. For example, a little word which breaks rapport very quickly is the word *but*.

"I totally agree with what you are saying, but . . . "
"I would like to buy your product, but . . . "

The *but* negates what has gone before. You are really communicating: "I don't agree with it", or, "I don't want to buy it, and here come my objections." Instead of tacking on these 'but' afterthoughts, try using the word 'and' instead. Although you may have to rearrange your sentence structure, you will be maintaining rapport.

Communicating with Mismatchers

A mismatcher is someone who disagrees with everything you say, on principle. The term, *polarity responder* is also used. Often you find that teenagers, in the process of asserting their own identity, take on a mismatching role – possibly so that they know *they* are deciding what to do, rather than have anyone else telling them. Sometimes this trait continues into adult life. These people will do the exact opposite of what you ask, or disagree with anything you say – on principle.

The best way to build rapport with someone who mismatches is to match them with your physiology and utilise their words. You take what they say, and put a polarity twist in it. With a determined mismatcher, you could say, "I don't think you will agree with me on this". And then add "But . . . " and say what you thought. They would probably respond, "Well, actually, no, I do", because they would want to mismatch you.

Once you have identified someone as a mismatcher, it becomes easy to communicate with them. You just need to frame things in this way:

"I don't think you will believe this. But . . . "
"I don't know that you will want to do this, but . . . "

With children you could say:

"I don't suppose you want to go to bed yet, do you?"
"No bed for you tonight!"

Consider your voice tonality as you say these sentences. You could use a tone of disbelief: "You can't do that", so that you will get, "Oh, yes, I can!" In which case you are helping them to get where they want to go anyway.

Embedded commands

Within any sentence, you can emphasise, or tonally mark out, any commands embedded in it. The commands in the sentences above are the verbs: *believe, do, go to bed.* You can use this in presenting and training by putting emphasis on what you want the audience to do. You are giving the command wrapped up or embedded in a longer sentence, so that it communicates more to the unconscious mind. In that way it is more likely to create compliance.

People use embedded commands all the time. In the following examples the embedded commands are underlined:

> "I don't know whether you want to <u>come to this training course</u>, but if <u>you do</u>, you need to <u>book now</u>."

People often do this negatively without noticing. For example, they say:

> "I'm not going to <u>put up with this</u> any longer."
> "Don't <u>forget to call me</u>."
> "The training room is down the corridor; you can't <u>miss it</u>."

The emphasis is on the opposite of what is wanted. Remember, the brain deals with negatives only after it has processed the positive command.

You may find it instructive to explore how embedded commands are used in this book. This is one of the secrets that has been in full view all the time!

Meetings with mismatchers

In meetings, no matter what ideas you come up with, mismatchers tend to present reasons why they won't work. They will see the downside of everything. Alternatively, if you say something won't work, they will come up with some reasons why it will.

In fact, this is a useful role in the group, especially if everyone else is very positive; you do need to check out possible obstructions, hazards and pitfalls. Mismatching is a useful skill to have, as long as it is handled productively. If it is happening continually throughout a meeting, ultimately nothing gets done. Once you have identified a mismatcher, limit their input to a specific time in the meeting. Frame this by explaining to them that during the meeting they have a special job to do:

> "Because you have this remarkable skill of finding out the little things that may prevent something from working, which could affect the success of the project, I want you to let us know what all those things are in the last five minutes of the meeting. Until then, all I want you to do is just listen and note them down."

They will then very likely say, "Oh, great. Thanks", because you are acknowledging them, rather than trying to shut them up. And they will cooperate because you are utilising their particular skill, which other people in the group don't have. This will completely transform your meetings, and your projects will progress. By flipping the communication the other way, everything becomes easier.

Matching voice tonality
You can also match someone's voice tonality. In a training you can simply provide examples using your own voice. On the printed page, the following descriptions will give you the relevant ideas to enable you to find auditory examples in your own experience.

Pitch: How high or low is the pitch of voice?
In physical terms, the pitch of the voice depends on the frequency of vibration of the vocal cords, which is determined by their length and mass. The greater the frequency of vibration, the higher the pitch. In the general population the range of pitch is about four octaves, from the deepest bass, to the highest soprano. An average untrained voice has a range of about two octaves.

Generally there is an overlap between the female frequency range and the male frequency range.

To get rapport you do not need to match the frequency exactly – fortunately. Whatever your natural voice pitch, moving in the direction of the other person's pitch will be sufficient to get rapport with them more easily.

For example, if you are a woman trying to match a deeper male voice, and you take on a low gruff voice, then they are likely to remember you, but not necessarily for the right reasons! Similarly, for a man wanting to match a higher female voice, speaking in falsetto is not going to get rapport for you! You will certainly get their attention, but that is probably not what you really want.

Figure 8.2: Comparative voice ranges

Get rapport by matching the *comparative* location within the range. If you are a woman wanting to build rapport with a man who is at the lower end of the male voice range (◉), by lowering your voice to the lower end of the female range (✹), you would still get rapport, even without matching the exact frequency. Likewise, for a man wanting to build rapport with a woman with a high pitched voice, moving toward the upper part of the male range would still get rapport for him.

To deepen or raise your voice in order to match someone else, all you need to do is put your attention lower down in your body or higher up in your head when you are speaking. That will naturally change the frequency of your voice. We will cover this in *Origins*, below.

Tempo: How fast or slow does someone speak?
There is wide variation in the tempo people use when speaking. Some people speak very, very slowly, and each word, it would seem, is ponderously brought up from the depths of thought. And other people, often those who work in the media, seem to chatter away at a furious rate, and you wonder just how many words they can get out without taking a breath. Information flies at you like machine gun fire.

So wherever you are starting from, slow down or speed up to meet their rate of speech. Mismatching someone who speaks slowly by using a 'hurry up' voice is not going to work!

Timbre: What is the quality, or resonance, of the voice?

Timbre is the overall quality of the voice. It is determined by the way in which the vocal cords vibrate, and how the voice resonates in the chest, throat, and mouth cavities. This varies enormously within the population. Some people may speak in a clipped, crystal-clear voice, with precise pronunciation. Others may be more breathy, slightly sibilant, or whisper confidingly. Yet others have harsh, grating, or scratchy voices, or sound rough, gruff, nasal, adenoidal or whining. If you were to match exactly, the other person would probably notice, and think you were making fun of them. Matching by moving toward their style will assist you in getting rapport.

Volume: How loud or soft do they speak?

As we grow through childhood we learn to control our vocal volume. Loud and soft are relative terms. Some people speak very quietly, so that even if you are in the same room, you almost feel like you have to lean forward to hear what they are saying. Conversely, other people project and fill any space with their penetrating voice. You may feel like whispering, "There's no need to shout!" Matching the level of the loudness of the voice, will enable you to establish rapport at an unconscious level.

Content chunks: How much do they say between breaths?

People parcel up their utterances in chunks, and vary how much content they'll put into each chunk before pausing.

Some speakers ... use small chunks ... and although ... they have ... long sentences ... they're broken up ... into small pieces ... using only ... so many words ... at a time. Whereas other people put quite a significant number of words together and often tend to run one sentence into another one before eventually taking a pause. So the content chunks are the number of words they string together before reaching a point where they take a natural pause for breath ...

Notice these variations in where people pause in their sentences to take breath, and then match this style of speaking.

Rhythm: Does someone speak in a monotone, or use a sing-song voice?

Speech rhythms are often related to geographical and cultural origin. We hear many different rhythms in the regions of the US and the UK as well as from English speakers around the world: the Caribbean, India, Australia, and so on. And there are individual differences in the way people put music into their voice. Some voices flow melodically, while others are halting and monosyllabic.

Some people have a standard structure for their utterances. And their voice follows the rhythm every time. So all of the sentences all follow the same sort of process. It is almost like the clickety-clack of a train. And it starts and then just carries on. And no matter what they want to say, it is just the same perpetual rhythm, that keeps on going all the time, throughout everything they say.

Picking up the same rhythm will enable you to get rapport with that person at the unconscious level. Again, move towards this rather than mimic, otherwise the other person will probably notice that you are not using your usual voice.

Origins: Which part of the body does the voice seem to come from?

The origin of the voice is where the voice starts from within the body. Ultimately it will come out of the mouth, but it doesn't originate there. This particular discrimination may seem unfamiliar, but is easy enough to learn.

Think of the body as three main zones: head, heart, and belly. Do this exercise inside for yourself:

Head
Focus you attention on your head area, and imagine your voice is coming from the middle of your head. How would it sound if you were to speak out loud?

The voice qualities from the head area are: higher pitch, slightly louder, quicker, clearer, more penetrating, and there is also a quality of lightness.

Heart
Now move your focus of attention to your heart area, to the middle of your chest, and have your voice originate there. How does it sound now?
Typical voice qualities from the heart area are: warmer, more resonant, middle frequency, slightly slower, and more inclusive.

Belly
Finally move your focus of attention down into your belly, below your navel, and have your voice come from there. And notice how that sounds.
Typical voice qualities from the belly area are: low pitch, slower pace, larger with an airy quality of space to it – more roundness, and more internal.

You can have your voice originate in any part of your body by imagining that place in your mind. Notice the quality of your voice when you let out the sound, and relate this to its origin inside you. Being familiar with these differences will give you clues on where someone else's voice originates in their body. You can then create your voice in the same place is your body. The more you practise this, the more aware you will become, and the finer the discriminations you can make. By creating your voice in different parts of your body, you will find that you will dramatically increase your flexibility in how your voice sounds. So if you are talking to someone and you notice, "Their voice is coming from their neck", and you put your voice in your neck area too, you will find that you automatically get rapport with them.

Where someone's voice comes from is probably related to other characteristics they have. These are explored in greater detail in Chapter Eleven.

Matching accents
Some people are natural mimics, and match voices and accents easily, while others maintain the voice they have grown up with.

If the other person has a strong regional or national accent, then, as a general rule, it is inappropriate to deliberately match that accent, even if you can do it perfectly, because you will blow the rapport – maybe not immediately, but when they find out you are really not from Scotland, or wherever it is, because they realise, "Something strange is going on". They may consider mimicking their accent to be insulting.

It's OK if you unconsciously take on accents, because that is not a deliberate attempt to match an accent – it naturally happens when you get into rapport with someone. However, if matching some-one else's voice is challenging for you, then start paying more conscious attention to your own voice, as well as other people's, so that you learn to make the necessary discriminations.

Exercise 7: Matching Voice Tonality

In this exercise you will be developing your matching ability. You need to be in a group of three. This is what you do:

- Two of you, A and B, are going to be sitting back to back. The third person, C, will be positioned so that they can hear both of you.
- A says a short sentence in their normal speaking voice. It could be the sentence they answer the phone with: "Hello", followed by their name, or whatever.
- B repeats the same words, and matches A's voice tonality: the pitch, speed, qualities, the origins, and so on.
- Keep doing this – A speaking, B copying – with the same sentence, until A gets the feeling of rapport inside of them. You will know when you have got it, because you will feel it. It kicks in, and instantly you know the other person has matched your voice. And B will get it as well. We don't know what it will be like for you, because everyone has their own personal calibration, but you will know when it is there. Keep going until you get it.
- Notice your own personal indicator for having rapport. It is useful to be familiar with the particular feeling that lets you know you have rapport, for example, when you are present-

ing to a group, or speaking to someone on the telephone, and you get the feeling, you know they have it as well.

- C's job as coach is to listen for key differences between the voice tonality of A and B, and to coach B in what they need to change to match even better. Give feedback to B on how they are doing. Remember the feedback sandwich, and say something like: "You're doing a great job, you have the same pitch, loudness and rhythm. The only thing you need to change to get an absolutely perfect match and get rapport, is to shift the origin . . . " Then have them do it again. And keep coaching them until they get the result.

Do this exercise now.

Debrief

You will find this is easier to do if you stop thinking about it, and just do it. Then it's easy, because you naturally do it anyway. It is just that you don't normally do it deliberately. We all have some capability for mimicry, and this is an opportunity for using your natural talent. If you start analysing the person's voice, you will overload yourself with too much information.

Match Posture

This need to analyse may happen more when you are in the coaching role. Because of the nature of and responsibility inherent in the coaching situation, you think: "I have really to get this right to assist the person." Instead, learn to trust yourself, and consider: "What is the one thing that, if they changed it, would enable them to get the result most easily?"

If you don't get it the first time, listen again. People's programs are very consistent over time.

With any form of rapport building, at first you need to go where they are. As soon as you get your indicator for rapport, begin to move back and lead them to where you normally speak from, and they will come with you, because they want to maintain rapport with you.

Exercise 8: Rapport with the Group

For the next exercise you need to be in a group of five or six.

- Take it in turns to stand up in front of your group. Your outcome is to build rapport with everyone in your group at the same time.
- For the audience: when you feel, or get your indicator that your presenter has rapport with you, and only then, raise your hand. If you feel that the rapport decreases or disappears, put your hand back down. Your hand is up only when you are getting your indicator that the presenter has rapport with you.
- As the presenter, your outcome is to get rapport with everyone in your group, to have everyone's hand up at the same time. That is how you know when you are done. You are not allowed to say anything, and you are not allowed to move around, though you may use some facial expressions and gestures if you wish.

Remember that everything you have done so far still counts. You still need to go into the trainer state, because that makes it much easier to get rapport with the group. You will know you have achieved this when everyone's hand is raised.

Do this exercise in your group now.

Debrief

Smiling definitely helps you achieve this. When someone smiles to you, it is an automatic response to smile back. Smiling makes a connection, because you have just matched them.

Once you have established the connection with a group, those people will be very forgiving. They want you to succeed. Should you be starting to panic: "What if I come out of trainer state? What if I forget what to say? What if I can't answer a question?" then provided you have that connection, people will allow you the time you need to return your attention to them. This is why it is so important to get that connection right at the beginning of a training or presentation, because then everything just flows.

Although there is a lot to do, this is a good example that less is more: the less you do, the more effective it is. For example, not moving or saying anything is not a restriction; it allows you to get the result more easily. In general, many people feel that when they are in front of an audience, they have to move around, to be busy doing something, to be seen to be working – otherwise they can't justify being there.

Being Totally Comfortable Doing Nothing

These exercises are designed to install the behaviours in you so that you do them automatically without thinking about them. You need to be totally comfortable in front of an audience, doing nothing, saying nothing, not moving. Because then, when you do start to move and say things, you can do them intentionally and achieve a much greater impact. The idea is that everything you do in front of an audience, whether it is one person, or 10,000 people, is done intentionally.

Once you are OK with deliberately doing nothing, then we can start adding layers. By the end of this book you will automatically be doing about 12 things in putting your message across. At this stage our outcome is to undo any of your current unconscious behaviours, so that we can put in intentional ones that will allow you to become a magical presenter.

Chapter Nine
Being Yourself

When first presenting, many presenters think, "It is not OK to be myself!" The more presenting we did, the more we realised that we got the best results when we were spontaneously being who we are, rather than doing any pretending. In any kind of training or presentation, being truly yourself is more than enough. In fact:

● *Being you is all you'll ever need.*

Most people need to let out more of who they really are. The more of you that is available to the audience, the more they will be able to connect and bond with you, and feel comfortable with you. Some relevant self-disclosure lets the audience get to know you as a person, rather than as a disembodied source of information. But this does not mean you have to reveal all of your private life to the audience. It means that you have to remove the barriers, so that the true you can emerge – the lively, spontaneous, playful, energetic self that you really are.

Remember in the previous chapter what happened in Exercise 5 where you silently matched the other person. When you have rapport with an audience, they will be in the same state as you. If you are agitated, or stressed, your audience will also start feeling that, but they won't know why. If you are balanced, calm, and OK about being yourself, they will feel balanced, calm, and OK about being themselves. Everything is then going to be much easier.

Fearful or comfortable?
If you have any fears about presenting, then the next thing is for you to let them go. First, you need to find out where you are right now on that score.

Of course, you may have no fear at all. Not everyone experiences fear about training or presenting. They never learned how to be fearful, so they calmly carry on presenting, totally balanced and comfortable.

You need to differentiate between feeling fearful and feeling excited. It is quite normal for even the most seasoned presenter to feel the rush of adrenalin just before they go on stage. And this helps them put more fire into their presentation or training. If you were totally relaxed or laid back, it might be difficult to impart any enthusiasm for your message and motivate anyone else.

Exercise 9: Self Assessment

How do you feel about being yourself in front of an audience? Be honest with yourself:

- Do you feel nervous, afraid, fearful, terrified, or petrified?
- Or do you take it in your stride, and enjoy the contact you have?

This could be true for any audience, or for only specific types of audiences.

Mark your current feeling on the grid:

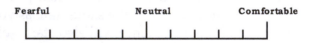

Letting go of fear
Have you ever had any kind of *inappropriate emotional responses* such as standing in front of an audience in a state of panic, or feeling petrified? You are definitely afraid, your hands are shaking, but this doesn't really make sense. Consider:

- What is the worst thing that could happen?
- What is the audience going to do to you?

They really want you to give of your best, so why would they want to be there otherwise?

If you have some limiting belief that gets in the way of your being totally comfortable being yourself in front of an audience, then it may be time to let that go. So how do you let go of a fear? Most fears are learned. This means you can also unlearn them. If you have made some unconscious decisions about being less than a totally magnificent, perfect, brilliant presenter or trainer, because of some fear, then it is possible to have your fears disappear, by first acknowledging that these fears are real, and have served you well over time. Then by getting the additional learning from those incidents where you learned to have the fear, you can then let the fear go. And in the future you can enjoy standing in front of any audience, being a better presenter or trainer because you are balanced, calm, and being yourself. So would it be worthwhile for you to let go of any limiting beliefs and any limiting decisions you might have made?

Limiting beliefs audit
Fear often disappears with familiarity. You may have been afraid simply because you had never done any presenting before. Having done some exercises, you are becoming familiar with what it is like to present successfully.

Earlier we talked about beliefs in terms of, "Whether you believe you can or you can't, you're right". Maybe you developed some beliefs regarding yourself as a presenter or trainer. So first of all, you need to identify any beliefs or decisions you made about being anything less than a totally magnificent and brilliant presenter and trainer. When you know what they are, accept that, "OK. That is how it was in those situations". Once you have acknowledged them you can do something about it – if you choose.

Here is what you do:

- Take the time to think about any limiting beliefs you have about being a presenter or trainer. Some beliefs may be near the surface, others quite deep, so you may find that some beliefs will pop up over an extended period of time. When they do, add them to your list.
- Identify the specific fears you have. Because you are coming at these consciously, it may seem, "This doesn't make

sense", but you cannot deny that your heart is racing, and your palms are sweaty, and so on. These are the kinds of responses you are looking for.

● Look again at the list of excuses you made at the end of Chapter Five. An excuse is a manifestation of an underlying belief. For example, by categorising other people as 'stupid' or 'slow learners' you are probably projecting onto them some aspect of yourself – possibly some inadequacy, perhaps that you are inflexible or lacking in knowledge on certain matters. Unpack any excuses, and turn them around so that you can own the belief from which it derives.

Exercise 10: Beliefs Audit Questionnaire

Answer the following questions to identify any limiting beliefs you may have:

What do I believe about:

● The venue itself, the physical setting?
This could be about presenting from a raised platform, from behind a lectern, having unreliable equipment.

● The people who make up audiences?
You may be OK presenting to people you don't know, but not to those you do know, or the other way around. Maybe you feel fear when you feel that the people are of higher status than you, or at a particular level within an organisation: managing directors, or CEOs, for example. Or you may be unhappy working with 'conscripts' – people who don't want to be there.

● The size of the audience?
Maybe you are OK with an audience of up to ten people, say, but not with 100.

● My past performance as a trainer or presenter?
Maybe you have a specific fear around not remembering all the material you are going to present, being at a loss for words, drying up on stage.

● My capabilities as a presenter or trainer?
  Maybe you are afraid of dealing with unexpected questions, or with 'difficult' people.

● What is possible and what is not possible for me?
  Complete some sentences that begin: "I can't . . . "; "I must . . . "; "I mustn't . . . "; and so on.

● Myself as a presenter or trainer?
  Maybe you think of yourself as unworthy, or inadequate in some way.

● Who I really am in front of an audience?
  Are you afraid of revealing 'too much' about yourself?

● Who I would be if I were to reveal more of myself when I am presenting or training?

● What am I assuming about the kinds of people there are in the world?
  What labels do you have for certain people or audiences, that fill you with dread, or cause you to lose your enthusiasm?

Whatever it is, notice what triggers the fear in you. There may be one thing, or many. If so, then identify the main fear, the one which, if you were to let it go or have it disappear, would have the biggest positive impact on your ability to demonstrate that you are a truly magnificent presenter and trainer.

When you have identified this key limiting belief, take the time to consider it. Acknowledge:

"This is just a belief. And there have been good reasons in the past for having had this belief, and it has served me well over the years.

"There are further learnings I can take from it.

"Now that I have fully acknowledged this belief, it is time to let it go . . .

"And I can have other beliefs that will support me, and allow me to become more of who I am, and be the excellent trainer or presenter that I can be."

Time Line Therapy®

Time Line Therapy® was developed by Tad James in the 1980s. It has a basic process which enables people to release any inappropriate emotional responses. Essentially fear comes from your unconscious mind, which is why it doesn't make sense. Your unconscious mind works on feelings and intuitions. Time Line Therapy works directly with your unconscious mind, though you will be guiding yourself through it with your conscious mind.

As far as the emotion of fear is concerned, you can be afraid of something only *after* it has occurred. Before it happened, you couldn't have predicted how you would respond. Fear is one possible reaction to what happened. When you anticipate a similar event happening again, you project the fear out into the future. You anticipate fear, based on past experience.

Have you ever been in a situation fraught with danger, and emerged from that predicament feeling relief or gratitude for safe deliverance? Immediately afterwards you were OK, totally balanced. It was only when you later recalled what you had been through that the fear came. Actually that is the way fear is supposed to work. It is a completely automatic response that kicks in only after the event has already happened, so that you know to get afraid. It is a message to avoid that situation in the future.

The time line is a useful metaphor for thinking about how you code time. It is an imaginary line connecting all the events in your life in the order they happened. In your mind you can travel anywhere in time. You can remember what you did last weekend, on your last holiday, unwrapping Christmas presents when you were a child, the last time you listened to a play on the radio . . . And you can explore any number of possible futures that you might wish to enjoy – including those in which you truly are a magnificent trainer or presenter . . . You have total flexibility exploring time in this way. Most people have their memories sorted chronologically such that can be represented as a continuous line.

When it comes to 'stage fright', 'performance anxiety', 'fear of public speaking', or whatever, there has to be a first event at some point on your timeline, after which you learned to be afraid of presenting in front of an audience. Otherwise you wouldn't know to do that. Generally, people are not born with stage fright. Many children really enjoy presenting themselves in front of an audience. Only at some later point do you develop the fear.

Exercise 11: Time Line Therapy® Techniques

By going back to that very first event, the one that made you afraid afterwards, you can do something about it. Here is the essence of the technique:

- Think of the first significant event, after which you became afraid. What would that event be?
- Then ask yourself: "15 minutes before the event started, where was the fear?" 15 minutes before the event started, there was no fear, because it couldn't be there.

Figure 9.1

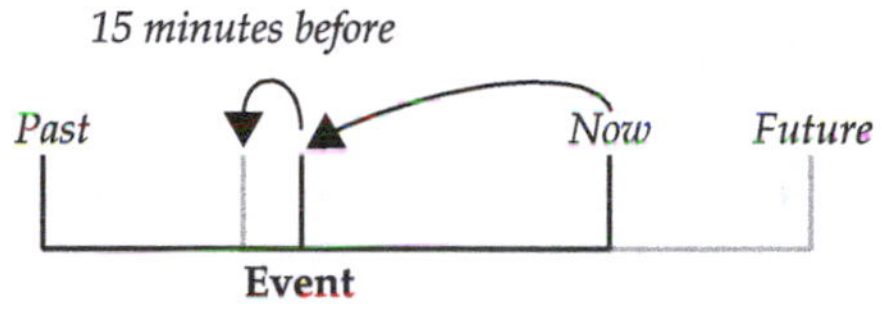

15 minutes before

Past   Now   Future

Event

Figure 9.1 shows various events along the timeline. The Time Line Therapy process is represented by the two arrows. Think back along the time line to that first significant event in the past, and then go back just a little further to a time before it all happened. And from that perspective, the memory will be different. By altering your perspective on any event in your mind, you will be changing your response to it.

Nothing to be Afraid of

Now, the reason you were afraid after that very first event is because there were certain things you didn't know then, but which you know now. If you had known them at the time, you wouldn't have been afraid. Often when you look back at those past events, you realise, "Actually my fears were groundless, there was nothing to be afraid of". For example, after David's earlier-described experience of 'attacking' the imaginary intruder, the knowledge that it was really the central heating cooling down took away the fear. But the adrenalin was still in the body – those feelings were real. David knew there was nothing to be afraid of, and that in future he would recognise those sounds and know what they were.

This is true for many incidents in your life, because you now know far more than you did then. By asking your unconscious mind to get all the learnings from that particular event, you will find that the fear disappears.

Sometimes when you ask your unconscious mind to find that very first event where you experienced fear of presenting yourself, you may not consciously know what it was. But your unconscious mind will know. So whether or not you know consciously what it was, just ask your unconscious mind to go back 15 minutes before that whole event. And from that place, notice: where is the fear? 15 minutes before the very first time you ever experienced fear, there was no fear. From that perspective it disappears.

Often when doing Time Line Therapy on yourself you may not actually be aware of what is happening in the event, but you get the result. The emotion you are working on disappears. Your unconscious mind knows what is happening there, but it might just choose not to let your conscious mind know. And you don't need to know, as long as you get the result.

Harvesting the Learnings

Before you let go of that event, and everything that it triggered in you afterwards, you need to get the rest of the learning from it. Once you have done that, your unconscious mind will be willing to let the fear go. So looking back from the safety of now, to that time 15 minutes before the event, with the resources and the understanding you now have, knowing that you survived, then you can simply go through that event again, consciously or unconsciously learning from it, and continue to grow as a person, as you come forward in time . . . until you are again in the present.

Your memory of that situation will now be different. Remember that every time you revisit a memory you change it in some way. Time Line Therapy techniques allow you to benefit from how your unconscious mind works. Once you have all of the learning from the event, the fear disappears. Your unconscious mind will recode the memory, allowing it to become a positive memory that you can use to build a new version of your future from that point on.

This may be a quite novel way of thinking for you. It may seem simplistic, possibly too easy. Maybe you have a limiting belief that change has to be difficult, requires a great deal of struggle and take ages . . .

When you think about changing your experience, you will know that this process makes some kind of sense, because you have done something similar many times already. Certain events in your past you have coded as negative, and others as more positive experiences:

● You made those decisions. And you can change them.

This is true because what you think determines what happens in your model of the world.

When you use hindsight to illuminate some aspect of your past, there is no need to hang on to any unnecessary emotional baggage. You can let all that go. It is often said that we have 20/20 vision when it comes to hindsight. You can make useful changes by recoding those memories as learning opportunities, and then your unconscious mind will revise your experience in the light of what you know now.

Chapter Ten
Energy

Working with Energy

In both presenting and training, one major difference in the way we work with groups is the way we use energy. Working with energy is a powerful way to change what happens within groups, and because you have greater awareness, you can be more flexible in what you do, and have more fun!

Every living creature has an energy field, which varies in intensity over time, but is always present to some degree. You can measure it with scientific instruments, and with Kirlian photography you can show that the state someone is in influences the energy field around them.

Have you ever met someone, and thought, "This person has a good energy. It feels great to be in their company". Or, alternatively, "Hey, what's with this person? I don't feel comfortable around them". Maybe you avoided them for no apparent reason, even though you didn't know them. Have you ever gone into a room and had the feeling, "Something happened here before I came in"? It is as though you have picked up some 'bad vibes', or sensed an 'atmosphere', because people had been arguing or fighting there. Alternatively you may have entered a room and sensed a feeling of well-being, relief, relaxation, or 'coming home'. Immediately your state changed, and you felt uplifted.

These types of experiences are the effects of your energy field interacting with other people's energy fields, and of the qualities of the energy that has been created in that place. Whenever a group comes together it generates its own 'group energy field'. Generally speaking most people aren't consciously aware of the energy emanating from others or from a particular physical space. Yet, unconsciously, you pick it up. One reason your mood or your state changes is because you are now interacting with other people's energy.

Controlling energy

This chapter is about exploring the energy you have in your own body, and the energy you put out, which affects other people. You will learn how to control your energy, the energy in the space around you, and the energy within the group to whom you are presenting.

So if you are already aware that you can instantly pick up the energy in a room, and that when people enter an energy field their mood changes, then what if you could set up the energy in the room the way you wanted it? What if you could customise the energy, the kind of feeling in the room, that would be most conducive to what you want to do there? For example, if you're having a sales presentation, or presenting some new business ideas, then what if you could set up the energy in the room for a state of curiosity, interest, or excitement, say, so that as soon as someone comes in they begin to feel curious, interested, or excited, even before you start your presentation? For a personal growth or self-development training, exploring group processes, you could establish an energy that produces a feeling of safety, transformation and change. Immediately people walk through the door, their mood begins to alter: they feel safe, and begin to change and transform themselves, simply because the energy in the room is in harmony with the results you want to create with those people. That would that be useful, wouldn't it?

Using energy means you are working on an almost invisible level with the people in your particular group. Using all of your training and presentation skills, you will learn to control the level of energy at the same time. And you will be able to do it whether or not the people in your group know this consciously. They may be aware at one level, perhaps just noticing a certain atmosphere in the room, or that the atmosphere has changed.

Looking after your own energy

It is essential to maintain your own level of energy. Once you know how to use this way of working with energy with others, you can also use it for yourself. When you have plenty of energy you can avoid those situations you probably had in the past where your energy ran low, you started tiring, and thinking:

"I don't have enough energy to do any more."
"I would be able to do a better job if I had more energy."

Many people have experienced this. What you are doing doesn't have to be physically strenuous. It could be dealing with other people, or anything demanding your attention or keeping you thinking. If you are a trainer or a presenter it might be:

"I've been presenting all day, and I'm exhausted."
"I've been training for five hours, and I am now flagging a little."
"It's been one thing after another, and I'm whacked!"

Other sources of energy
We're going to teach you how to maintain your energy level, so that when you are presenting in front of an audience, instead of using up your own energy, you can use the energy that is naturally all around you to keep going all day. Then, at the end of the day, rather than feeling tired, you'll feel as though you have more energy than when you started. It means that when you get home you'll have energy for doing other things, rather than collapsing in a chair, sighing, "Phew! I'm wiped out".

Energy work exercises
The next three exercises provide direct experience of using energy, so that you will know more about how to work with the energy systems in your body. We also want to teach you about focusing your attention, because where you focus your attention has a dramatic effect on both the energy in your body, and your physical balance.

These exercises demonstrate that where you put your mental attention actually changes your physical body. They are examples of the mind-body connection. We firmly believe that the mind and the body are intimately connected, that they act as a system, and that one way into that system is through what you are paying attention to.

Do these exercises with a partner to explore how this mind-body connection works. Read through all the instruction and study the photographs first, so that you will be able to safely do the same thing with your partner.

Figure 10.1

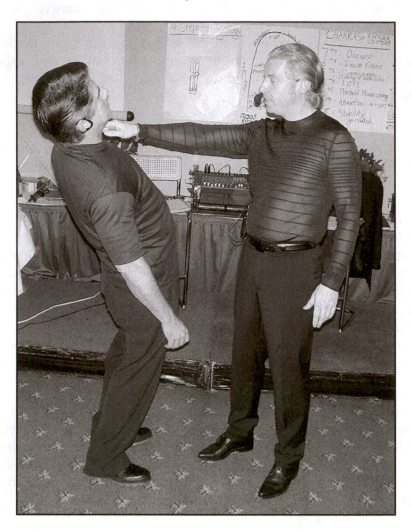

Exercise 12: Attention and Balance

● Tell your partner: "Place all of your attention, all of your mental attention, in your right earlobe." They focus on their right earlobe just by thinking about it and by putting all of their attention right inside it. Check that they are completely focused on their right earlobe by asking them: "Are you there?"

● Find out how balanced your partner is by gently pushing on their shoulder. Push from the front, straight toward them (*Figure 10.1*). You will discover that the lightest touch is enough to push them off balance. They move backwards, become unstable, start to wobble or even fall. When they are totally focused on their right earlobe, they are physically unbalanced – literally a pushover.

● Next tell your partner: "Imagine a large sphere or a ball of energy in your belly area, in the centre of your body, just below the navel. And now put all of your attention in this area." They shift their attention down in their body, to this area below their navel, which, in the martial arts disciplines, is called the *energy centre* or *power centre*. In Tai Ji, it is the *dan tien*, in yoga it is the *hara*; many names for this place in the middle of your body, a few inches below your navel. Check with them: "Are you down here?"

● Do the same test again. Push their shoulder and notice the difference. In *Figure 10.2* we are actually pushing much harder, and David's partner is still quite balanced. Although their shoulder moves back, they are twisting the body more. And as soon as the pressure is released they will swing back again as though they are on a spring. They are far more flexible this time.

Take turns doing this exercise with a partner. Notice what happens when you change your focus of energy from your earlobe to your belly or centre.

Debrief

When people do this, they notice their balance is completely different as a result of shifting their mental attention down into the belly. Now the thing about this is as follows.

● If you continually focus your attention down in your centre when you are presenting, then not only will you be physically balanced, but you will also be balanced in other ways.

Figure 10.2

For example, if while you were presenting someone asked you a difficult question, or you had a heckler in the audience, or some disruption threw you off balance, then the reason you were thrown off balance is because your attention shifted away from your centre, and onto the person asking the difficult question, or to the distraction, or whatever. As you lost your mental balance, you also lost your physical balance. Maybe the reason you couldn't come up with an answer, or you didn't know how to handle the heckler, was because you were no longer balanced, mentally or physically.

When you notice you are becoming off-balance, simply bring your attention back down and focus it in your centre. Go back into the trainer state, rebalance yourself, and check your breathing, before doing anything else. It's OK to pause, and have the audience wait for you. Only answer the question, or handle what is happening in the group when you are balanced and centred again. This can be a very quick thing to do; we are talking about only a few seconds .

Exercise 13: Let's Twist Again . . .

This exercise also demonstrates that what you are doing in your mind, where you are putting your attention, affects your body. You may do this on your own, but it is easier to do with a partner.

- Stand behind your partner and say to them: "Put your left arm out straight in front of you. Now, keeping your arm out straight, twist the upper part of your body from the waist, and twist as far around to the right as you can comfortably go." When your partner twists around, mark the position of greatest rotation by standing in that place where their arm stopped moving (*Figure 10.3*).

- Now tell your partner: "Now go back to the resting position. And just in your mind's eye, I want you to visualise or imagine twisting again. But this time you are imagining twisting a lot further round." In your imagination you can twist the whole 360 degrees, and more! There are no physical constraints to what you can imagine doing in your mind's eye. If you have watched cartoons, or movies like *The Exorcist*, you will know many things are possible!

- Ask your partner to repeat that visualisation in their mind a couple of times, until they can fully imagine twisting far further. When they have done that, say: "Now actually twist physically. Twist your body, and notice how far your arm goes this time."

Figure 10.3

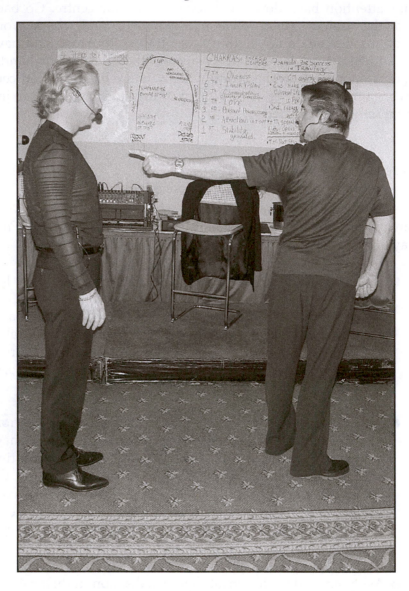

And notice how far their arm goes back around the second time (*Figure 10.4*).

Do this experiment now with your partner, and notice what happens as a result of doing the visualisation first.

Figure 10.4

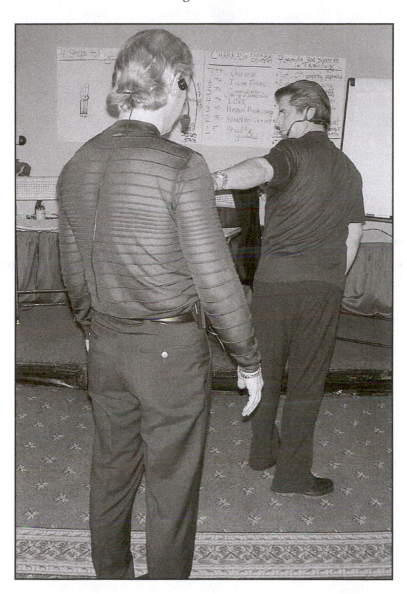

Energy Follows Thought

This is another example of energy following thought. The result of visualising this action before doing it is that the arm rotates further. Flexibility in your mind manifests in greater flexibility in your body – which indicates that your mind and your body are inextricably linked; they are one system, rather than two separate systems.

You may want to experiment with other aspects of consciously directing your attention. For example, what would happen if you take the learning from Exercise 12, and use it in this exercise? Putting your attention down in your centre and then in your mind see yourself twisting even further, then with your body you may find you rotate even further. Try this for yourself and notice what happens.

Exercise 14: The Unbending Arm

In this exercise it is better if your partner is about the same physical size and strength as you. This is the procedure:

- Stand facing your partner, at arms length from them, and put your right arm on your partner's left shoulder. If you are right handed, use your right arm; if you are left-handed use your left arm. Rest the back of your wrist on their shoulder, with your elbow downward, so that it can bend under pressure.
- Have your fingers clenched in a fist.
- Your partner clasps both hands over your elbow joint.
- When you are ready, they use their physical strength to pull down, bending your arm. As they do this, you resist by using your physical strength to keep your arm straight. (*Figure 10.5*).
- Notice how much effort it takes to attempt to keep your arm straight.

When you are in the arm bending role, notice how much pressure you need to apply in order to bend the other person's arm.

What usually happens when you do this is that your arm bends at the elbow under the applied force, because of the way the levers in the arm work. When such a force is applied, you cannot hold your arm straight with muscle strength alone.

Figure 10.5

Figure 10.6

Now do this again, but this time imagine that ball of energy in your centre.

- This time your hand, resting palm up on their shoulder, is open, with your fingers straight out.
- In your imagination, visualise you are generating energy in your centre, down in your belly. Imagine this energy flowing up through your body, into your shoulder, along your arm,

and out through your fingertips. With your hand open and fingers splayed out, imagine energy streaming from your fingers and disappearing into the infinite horizon.

- You may want to imagine the energy as white light streaming out of the end of your fingers, going all the way to the very furthest reaches of the universe.
- As soon as you have that visualisation running in your mind strongly and consistently, tell your partner to bend your arm again. And notice what is different this time (*Figure 10.6*).

Do both parts of this exercise now with your partner, and notice what happens as a result of shifting your attention.

Debrief

The first time your arm bends under pressure. The second time, even though the other person tries hard, they fail to bend your arm. Your arm stays straight not because you have suddenly built some more muscles, or the other person is getting tired. It stays straight as a result of visualising the flow of energy. You also have a very different physiology, with no strain or stress – which is very different from using your physical strength.

When you are the person applying the pressure, the first time your partner is probably straining and using a lot of effort. The harder they resist, the more their face shows the effort they are making. The second time, you notice that their face and the rest of their body is much calmer and relaxed, almost as though there is no need for any effort or strain at all.

Again, you might like to experiment with what else would help you to do this. For example, you may find you have greater stability by having your energy connect you strongly to the ground. Imagine that you are sending down roots into the centre of the Earth and connecting with all that energy.

If in the first part of this exercise, you found that as you were reacting against your partner pulling down on their arm, it was as though your body started rising up, or you were being lifted off the ground, then counteract that by moving your attention down to your feet, as though you are planting yourself in the earth. By grounding the force being applied to you, it loses its impact on your body. Your arm will stay rigid, and you will remain in place. This is very different from resisting someone else's force by using your physical strength alone.

Some people, when they do this exercise, get concerned that they might be depleting their energy resources. If this is true of you, just imagine energy coming from outside of your physical body, for example, from deep within the earth, from the sun, or from the sky and beyond.

Others fear that their energy might be dissipated and lost, so they don't fully visualise it leaving their fingers – or at any rate going very far, and certainly not to the infinite horizon. However, by inhibiting the flow you may get the feeling that there is a restriction or blockage and the arm is filling up, or getting congested.

Building up energy
Perhaps you are wondering:

- How can I ensure I have enough energy?
- How can I build up greater energy resources?
- How can I access other sources of energy, so that I'm not using up all of my own?

If so, you need to know how to build up greater reserves of energy, and how to draw energy from elsewhere.

We often do longer trainings: seven days, or 16 days, and often run them consecutively, so we may be on stage for up to 36 days with only a couple of days off in the middle. Every day we might be training from 10 o'clock in the morning till 8 o'clock in the evening. People sometimes ask: "Where do you get all your energy? I'm just sitting in the audience, yet I am feeling exhausted. And you're up there with loads of energy, still delivering the stuff."

Being on stage 200 days a year requires a lot of energy, so we need to make sure we have sufficient reserves to do that. Using the techniques here ensures that by 8 o'clock in the evening, you will actually have extra energy at the end of the day. Our students who have learned these techniques tell us that they also have more energy at the end of the day. Even at the end of 36 days training, we always have more energy than we had at the beginning. That means we can enjoy the rest of our life. It is important that people enjoy other activities apart from their career or job.

Having more energy means you will have a richer life and gain more pleasure from it. This is more than just having increased energy to do presentations and trainings. You can have more energy whenever you want it, any time, whatever you do. Even if you are working with clients on a one-to-one basis, which many therapists and practitioners find tiring, you can learn how to create reserves of energy. We each have a busy therapy practice, often seeing clients, without a break, for in excess of ten hours a day. Again, we feel energised at the end of it, by using these particular energy techniques.

Everything is energy

So where does energy come from? Actually, everything in the universe is energy: we are made of energy; we are alive with energy. All living creatures have a biological energy, which some people call the life force. We often refer to thinking as using our mental energy. So how do you tap into this energy so that you can use it?

Well, you have already been tapping into it inside yourself by focusing your attention. When you focused your attention and started directing the flow of energy through your arm, it had a profound effect on your physical body. You were using energy that is a resource inside you. When you become aware of the amount of energy within you, you can focus it in a particular direction, with a specific intention, and you give it specific qualities.

Huna and energy

You increase the energy in your body through something that we all do all the time, but were never taught how to do properly – breathing.

In *Huna*, the ancient teachings of the Hawaiian people, we learn that they were very concerned with energy and their personal energy levels. Their basic belief was that if someone was unwell, either mentally or physically, it was because they didn't have enough energy. By giving them enough energy again, they would get well. And one way to get enough energy was through breathing – but breathing in a particular way.

You also get energy through what you eat. We know this, but we often do not heed the evidence of our own eating behaviour. Our culture thrives on producing diets for healthy eating, and so on, and there is a wide range of diets available. As a result we all know some general nutritional principles of what it means to eat healthily, although we hardly ever consider the effect of eating on our energy level.

Someone once asked: "Has there ever been a Hawaiian Huna diet book?" We said, "We don't think a Huna diet book would sell very well. And we doubt whether you would get a publisher". Because the ancient Hawaiian guidelines on diet would be:

- If you eat it and you have less energy afterwards, then don't eat it any more.
- If you eat it and you have more energy afterwards, then eat more of it.

It doesn't really make for interesting reading. But it does make a lot of sense.

What if we were to consider that an important part of eating healthily was based on how we feel after eating in terms of our energy level. Think of the things you eat, which, after you have eaten them, make you feel drowsy, or even fall asleep. And there are other foods, which after you have eaten them, make you feel more awake, more alert, and have more energy. Of course, if you never feel like this, then maybe you need to check your diet!

The Hawaiians would also say:

- If you have a particular behaviour, or you do some particular action, and at the end of it you have less energy, then stop doing it.
- If you have a particular behaviour or do a particular action, and it results in having more energy, then do more of it.

If you want to ensure that you are building up your energy, if you always want to keep your energy levels high, and have more energy all the time, then check your breathing, your eating, and your behaviour. Then you will always have more energy than you will ever need.

We started exploring breathing as Step 4, *Pranayam*, of the trainer state. Increasing your energy comes from breathing in a particular way. You are going to do some breathing in which the ratio of the outbreath to the inbreath is two to one. In other words, you take at least twice as long to breathe out as to breathe in. The Hawaiians called this kind of breathing the *Ha breath*. By breathing this way, and especially by breathing from the diaphragm, which is at the bottom of your ribcage, you will increase the amount of energy in your body. With diaphragmatic breathing, your stomach goes in and out – which is one way to check that you are breathing from there. To check your own breathing, put your hand on your stomach, below the ribs, and breathe so as to move your hand.

Exercise 15: Ha breathing

Let's do some Ha breaths. This will be easier if you are standing up, with your feet firmly on the floor. So take your shoes off, and plant your feet so that they are about shoulder width apart and you are balanced with your weight equally distributed on each leg.

This is how you do Ha breathing:

Breathe in deeply through the nose.

When you breathe in this way, your stomach should come out. You can put your hand there to provide feedback. As you breathe in, your lungs fill, your diaphragm moves down, and your stomach comes out.

As you breathe out your diaphragm goes back up again, and your stomach goes in.

So take another deep breath in through the nose . . .

Exhale, out through the mouth: *ha-ah* . . . Actually make that long ha-ah sound.

And again, breathe in . . . and out: *Ha-ah* . . .

and again, breathe in . . . and out: *Ha-ah* . . .

and again, breathe in . . . and out: *Ha-ah* . . .

Just by breathing this way a few times, your energy increases. People often report certain shifts inside, such as feeling lighter, more relaxed, more grounded, more at home.

Whenever the practitioners of Hawaiian Huna, the *Kahuna*, were going to do anything together – and they were well-known for achieving tremendous feats of healing, both physiologically and psychologically – the first thing they would do would be to breathe together like that, sometimes for as long as six hours continuously. You can imagine how much energy they would have from doing that!

You do not need to do this for the full six hours in order to have plenty of energy to take you through the day. You will get the benefits by doing this for only a few minutes. A good time would be 20 minutes or for however long is comfortable for you.

When doing Ha breathing on a training, we will be linking the breathing with some Hawaiian visualisation techniques. We will also be having people moving their energy around, focusing it, putting it in certain places, and adding selected qualities into the energy around you.

Personal charisma

One manifestation of Ha breathing is an increase in personal charisma. You may have thought that charisma was something people either have or they don't. So what do we mean by charisma? You may have encountered certain people who set you thinking: "There's something about that person. They have an 'aura' around them, a lot of personal magnetism." That is charisma. As soon as you are near them, you are aware of their presence in an almost tangible way. When they enter a room it is almost as though their presence gets there a few seconds before their body. Have you ever met anyone like that?

You can actually increase your own personal charisma through breathing. It is a learnable skill. What you may call a person's presence, their magnetism, their aura, or their personal charisma, comes from having more of the kind of energy we have been talking about. By increasing the amount of energy you have in your body, and by moving it out from your body into the space around you, you will increase your own personal magnetism.

You have probably experienced this energy flowing out from people. Have you experienced the sensation that someone is staring at you from behind? Maybe you had the feeling their eyes were boring into you. Perhaps you felt compelled to turn around and look for the source of that sensation. You turned around and you looked straight at them, as if you already knew where they were. So how did you know who was looking at you? What let you know that they were looking at you?

As soon as you start paying someone a lot of attention, your energy follows that attention, and the person whom you are focusing on unconsciously picks it up. They have the feeling someone is looking at them, and they turn round. Their unconscious mind already knows where the source of that attention is, so they look straight at you. This is a similar process to projecting your energy, increasing your charisma or personal magnetism. The difference is you have more energy available, and you are putting your attention into more of the space around you, and now there is more for other people to become aware of.

Exercise 16: Energy Breathing

To do this breathing exercise, and explore putting out energy, you need to be standing up. You are also going to be doing some physical movements with the breathing, in order to circulate the energy around, so find a space where you can move easily. It would be even better doing this out of doors. Wherever you are, we suggest you have open space in front of you, so that you can look into the distance.

As you do this, you can be standing in front of the group so that they are able to watch you in their peripheral vision. Here you need to study the movements from the accompanying photographs beforehand (*Figures 10.7–10.8*).

Figure 10.7

Figure 10.8

This is what you do:

- Take off your shoes, so that you have greater contact with the ground.
- Standing on the floor, move one foot about one pace in front of the other. Balance your weight equally on both feet, unlock your knees so that they bend slightly, and then focus your attention on your centre, just below your navel, so that you can then lower your centre of gravity. As you do that, your body sinks slightly. You may have seen people doing *tai chi*, the ancient Chinese movement meditation exercises, in the park. This movement comes from *tai chi*. We came across this breathing pattern and the physical movement

during our study of Huna. Since then we found that it has many parallels to *tai chi* as well as to Yoga.

- Looking straight ahead, extend both arms forward, with your palms forward, and lean forward (*Figure 10.7*). Breathe in fully through your nose, and at the same time pull the energy towards you. Imagine pulling energy in with both hands, by grasping lightly, and then bringing your fists in toward your chest. As you do this, your weight naturally shifts to the rear leg. Imagine the energy coming inside you and filling your chest.

- Then breathe out through your mouth, and as you do that, just imagine the energy filling your body, and then expanding into the space around you. At the same time, push out using your hands, palm forward, expanding your energy field in front of you. You will naturally shift your weight onto your forward leg (*Figure 10.8*). At the end of the cycle, rotate your wrists and close your fingers, ready to start again.

- Repeat this whole inbreath and outbreath cycle several times, to familiarise yourself with the pattern. With every breath you take in you are drawing energy into your chest, storing the energy within your body; and with every breath out you are extending your energy field around you, pushing your hands forward as you lean slightly forward.

OK. Take a brief rest. In a moment we suggest you do this breathing cycle for about 20 minutes (or as long as is comfortable for you at this time). To remain comfortable, feel free to change your leg positions and have a different foot in front whenever you need to. And when you are ready again, stand in this posture, and start the breathing cycle in order to increase your energy.

Do the Ha breathing exercise now for between five and 20 minutes.

Debrief

You are going to feel rather different at the end of doing this breathing exercise. Do this breathing every day if possible, or whenever you need to build your energy. You don't need to do it for 20 minutes every time. Just five minutes in the morning and five minutes at night would give you far more energy than you currently have. It seems to wake you up in the morning, and relax you to go to sleep at night.

When preparing for a presentation, we suggest you do this for at least ten minutes. You can do it just before you go down to the training room. Or, if you're driving from another place to the training, you can do it when you first get up in the morning. Ten minutes of breathing is good before doing a presentation. And then, when you have that amount of energy, you will notice that everything goes completely effortlessly as the energy is flowing.

If you are not used to breathing like this, then at first you may feel the results of the energy building up in your body. If you start feeling dizzy, it means you are building up too much energy in your head. Then all you need to do is move the energy down in your body into your belly, to your centre area.

If you are unused to physical exercises like this, holding the muscles in that position for that amount of time may start your legs vibrating. Or you experience your joints aching, and so on. But if at any point you feel a little dizzy, or your legs are aching, or whatever, just stand in your centred position, doing nothing. Then as soon as you are feeling balanced again, resume the breathing with the body movements. The more you do this, the easier it gets.

We suggest you start doing this standing up so that you are learning the whole body breathing pattern. Once you are used to doing it standing up, it is perfectly OK to vary your position. You can even do the breathing sitting down, and you most likely will be if you are meditating. When you are sitting down make sure you have both your feet flat on the floor and your spine upright. We prefer to do it standing up with the physical movements when doing presentations because it's important to get the energy moving around. The physical movement helps get the energy flowing.

You can also put desirable qualities into the energy you are sending out. So think about the qualities you would like to have in the space around you. You may have anything you like, such as curiosity, safety, fun or joy. These would be good for training or presenting. All you have to do is to imagine putting that quality into the energy you are sending out.

With every breath out, push that energy into the room. You may find this easier if you give the energy a colour and a sound. And then just push it out so that everybody in the room who comes into touch with that energy begins to feel curious, or safe, or have a feeling of fun or joy.

Harnessing the energy in a group
The next exercise is about the energy in a group. So just to remind you of one of the concepts:

- *Energy follows attention.*

Wherever your attention goes, your energy flows. As you put your attention on something or someone, your energy moves to that place, or to that person.

In that experience where someone is looking at you from behind, and you turn around and they are staring at you, then you know they are paying attention to you. This means that the way people in a group know you are paying attention to them, is because they consciously or unconsciously sense your energy. Your energy is flowing toward them because you have your attention on them. Therefore one of the quickest ways of connecting with a group of any size is to set up that energy flow, because it will enable you to quickly get a connection with them.

Exercise 17: Connecting with the Energy of the Group

Get with your group, and have them sitting in an arc in front of you, as in *Figure 10.9*. You are standing in position x.

Figure 10.9

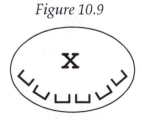

This is what you do:

- First of all go into the trainer state.

- In your mind's eye, imagine your energy, and push that energy out so that it goes beyond the farthest person. Put your energy right out behind the group, and around behind you. Be in peripheral vision to include everyone in the group, so that your attention is on everyone, and your energy is flowing to everyone at the same time.
- Now imagine pulling that energy field in just a little bit. Imagine putting out a ring of energy behind the whole group, and then tightening it just a fraction.
- For people in the group, as soon as you feel the connection with, or the energy from, the person up in front, then please put your hand up, (as you did in the rapport exercise earlier). And if you feel the energy disappear, put your hand back down again.
- As presenter, your outcome is to have all the hands up at the same time. And you are going to achieve that through connecting with your audience in terms of energy. And notice how this differs from when you did it before in the rapport exercise.

Again, for this exercise, you are just going to be standing still, centred, in front of your group, thinking and directing your energy. Of course you can move your head, your face, and you can move your eyes too. That's all. So relax, and be naturally standing in a balanced position. There is no need to be walking around.

This is the last exercise where you have to stand still and be silent. The reason for this is that we want you to know that you can pick up the whole group while just standing still.

Do this exercise now, and find out how this works for you.

When you have done it, take a moment to consider: What did you learn, what did you discover, what questions do you have, about that exercise?

Debrief

People are often surprised that this works, because they find that they get almost all of the group the first time. Sometimes they stand there and they do it and all the hands go up, and they think to themselves, "Hang on a minute, that can't be right!" But it is. Using this technique makes it easy. However, you must be in peripheral vision.

Sometimes all you need to do is take your time, go into the trainer state, and allow yourself to smile. Having a real warm, easy smile will be a good move. The quality of your energy will change when you smile, because you have changed your state. And thinking is not necessary. Remember the slogan: "Stop thinking: come to your senses." As the number of things to do increases, you won't have time to think. You are just going to have to go into it. So you are just going to have to leave any fears or nervousness behind and get on with it. Stop thinking; just do it – then it will work.

Doing this around a table

This method will still work around a table, because the energy will still be flowing to where your attention goes. So if you are sitting around a table, you need to put your attention on everyone at the table. You might have to be in peripheral vision, because some of them may be on either side of you. But as soon as you pull in your awareness all the way around, you will get the same effect.

As an example of the other extreme, we have used this particular process with a group of five or six hundred people, and we got a very quick connection with 99% of the people in the room, certainly within five minutes. And obviously you need peripheral vision because you can't even see the faces of the people at the back, so you have to just roll it out, as it were, as far as the back of the auditorium. So if you remember that your energy flows where your attention goes, then no matter what layout you have, it will work.

The other thing about your energy flowing to where your attention goes, is that the person you are paying attention to doesn't even have to be in the room. So if you have had one of those instances when you think of someone and then the phone rings, and it is the same person, that explains how it works. Space is not a problem as far as that is concerned, because in energy terms, location doesn't exist.

This works on the telephone as well. If you imagine you are actually with the person to whom you are speaking, paying attention to them, they will probably sense your presence, and feel that you are almost in the room with them. When you are on the phone, see the person, and put your awareness in the room with them. Even if you have never seen them before, guess what they look like, and imagine talking face-to-face with them. You will certainly get more of their attention and find it easier to build rapport.

Adapt and modify this technique for your particular context. It will work with any audience, of whatever size, in any environment, and over any distance, so that you will be connecting with your audience and they will be experiencing this connection with you. That gives you a basis for getting your message across to them. Unless and until you build that connection, you may be wasting your time, at least with some of the people in the audience.

Chapter Eleven
The Five Senses and Your Language

Getting your Message across

Although there will be some people who just want to be at your training or presentation because they respect you as a presenter – they know they are going to learn something useful and be entertained at the same time – the main reason people turn up is because they are interested in the content of your message – they want to hear what you have to say. Therefore the words you say are important. And you need to make sure that the words are working for you in getting your points across. Otherwise your message may get lost.

Exercise 18: Incident – Point – Benefit

From now on you will be using words in the exercises. To start with you will be telling one of the short stories you have been gathering throughout your life. The kind of story you need here is a very brief anecdote that lasts for less than a minute.

In order to produce the greatest benefit to the audience, you must structure the content of what you plan to say. The incident – point – benefit exercise is one way of providing structure; it will assist you in keeping to the point, and getting your message across clearly, so that people know what's in it for them. But before you start to say anything, you still need to be in the trainer state, connect with your group, establish rapport, and so on. This time, if you wish, you can move your body, although you may choose to find out what it is like if you stand still.

This is what you do:

- Stand in front of your group and tell them about a particular incident. Give them an account or tell them a story of something that happened to you, or you have heard about, or that you have made up. It can be anything at all, but there has to be some point you are wanting to get across to them – which is why you are bothering to tell them about it.
- Tell them the point that you want them to get: "And the point of this is . . . "
- And finally, tell them the benefit for them in getting the point. "And the benefit for you is . . . " It is important that it is the benefit for them, rather than the benefit for you.
- You have just one minute to do all of this: tell *them* about an incident, make your point, and give them the benefit of them getting the point.

Thinking in this way focuses your mind. When first presenting, it would be easy to ramble on for half an hour, without getting any points across at all. So if you can do this in one minute, then in 30 minutes you can get across 30 incidents, with their points and the benefits for the audience. You are getting your message across, point by point. And they know it is worth hearing, because you are telling them all the benefits.

The incident you talk about can be anything at all. It doesn't have to be true. It may or may not be related to anything you normally talk about when you are training or presenting. This is more about the process than the content.

Do this exercise now, taking turns to tell one incident – point – benefit each.

Debrief

That last exercise is much easier if you are consciously doing the incident – point – benefit, and unconsciously doing all the rest of it. Because the most you can hold in your conscious mind is between five and nine things. You already have to think about:

outcome, posture, the trainer state, energy, rapport, peripheral vision, and tonality . . .

In the 1950s the psychologist George A Miller did some research on human information processing. He discovered that on average the maximum amount of 'information' that people can deal with is about 7 ± 2 bits of information. That is to say, they can consciously hold between five and nine things in their mind at one time. After they have reached their limit or 'channel capacity', they go into a state of confusion or overwhelm, and cannot handle any more information without making mistakes.

What we do is to group or chunk information as we learn it. Remember learning to drive a car. At first our channel capacity was being stretched to the limit because there are more than a dozen things to pay attention to. But gradually, we chunk related smaller parts of the experience into larger units such as 'changing gear', 'signalling our intentions', and so on. Then we chunk even more, so that we know how to park, negotiate all types of turns, join freeways. Over time we developed huge chunks such as 'driving to work'. As skills become more unconscious, we can concentrate on larger chunks. The same process is true in learning any physical and mental skill, such as dancing: first learning how to place and move your feet, then joining sequences of steps, until you know the whole dance.

Most people are overloaded when they are doing an important training or a key presentation. Therefore you need to have all the techniques in place first, so that you can do them automatically. This is the point of doing these exercises. You are installing a pattern of behaviour that will work for you, as long as you just do it. When you start thinking about everything, things start not going perfectly. It is just your conscious mind that is overloaded. So focus your conscious mind on your outcome, the purpose of the exercise, and just allow your unconscious mind to do everything else.

Different Ways of Processing Information

The next step for you is to discover your own preferred style for processing information. And you will also learn about other people's styles, which may be the same, or quite different from yours.

One important understanding to come out of NLP is how it is possible to have different ways of thinking, and different ways of doing things. We each have unique models of the world, and NLP offers a large number of useful distinctions at a very basic, content-free level. For example, some people prefer to see things, and others prefer to touch, whatever these things are. Before we become aware of the huge variability of human experience, we may think that people are pretty much all the same. But the more we learn of these distinctions, the more we realise how fundamentally different people really are. And then we may begin to wonder how it is possible that we communicate at all!

Representational Systems

In Chapter Two, we said that at any moment there are only six things you could be doing inside your head: seeing pictures, hearing sounds, having feelings, talking to yourself, smelling or tasting. The ones we are interested in here are the first four: pictures, sounds, feelings and self talk. These are the most dominant representational systems in our culture.

We can all do all four, but generally people use one representational (rep) system more than the others. The one we find easiest to use is called our *preferred* representational system. Some people prefer thinking in pictures, some in sounds, some in feelings, and others in words – in self-talk or logical analysis. We like to receive information presented to us in the particular form that matches our preferred rep system. In any group, there is likely to be a mixture of all four preferences. They are probably not evenly distributed, but each is present to some degree.

Visual preferred system

When communicating to these people on a one-to-one basis, then use visual language, show them pictures, videos, brochures illustrated with photographs or diagrams, and tell them how things look from your point of view. 'Paint pictures' with your words:

"How do you see this? Can you picture this scenario? What do you envision? Keep an eye on this, get the whole picture, and then just give me the highlights."

Visual words

see	look	hazy	observe	flash
view	picture	misty	image	show
vision	focus	glimpse	glowing	sparkle
colourful	scan	gaze	brilliant	highlight
outlook	perspective	glitter	vivid	bright
insight	dawn	illuminating	shine	transparent
reflect	murky	go blank	scene	opaque
watch	appear	envision	lacklustre	mirror
show	reveal	crystal clear	dim	snap shot

Auditory preferred system

These people notice how things sound. They like listening to people talking to them, telling them stories, either live, or on audiotapes. They are attuned to voice tonality, which may be music to their ears, or sound hollow, or even tongue-in-cheek. They listen out for others speaking their language. Make sure your communication sounds good to them: play them music, or jingles, use a rich voice tonality, and talk to them using words to do with sounds:

"How does this sound to you? Does it strike a chord? Are you tuned into these themes? Sound these people out. Find out if they are on your wavelength."

Auditory words

hear	say	speak	shrill	loud
listen	click	talk	cacophony	whisper
sound	resonate	amplify	noise	discordant
tone	rhythm	screech	quiet	cadence
accent	harmony	dialogue	melody	symphony
musical	tune in	raucous	buzz	tell
call	clash	ring	shout	echo
tune out	be all ears	chime	announce	babble
jingle	mellifluous	discord	mute	sniff

Kinesthetic preferred system

These people have more of a feeling for things, use a hands-on approach, so they can grasp the essentials while sifting through a mass of information. They are fascinated and challenged with how things fit together, by organising the stuff someone has dumped on them. No need to handle them with kid gloves: make contact by physically touching them, and use language that touches on feeling words, you won't get the brush off:

> "Do you have a feel for this? Does it grab you? Put your feelers out. Dig down. Get hold of the essence. And give me your impression, so that I can get a handle on it."

Kinesthetic words

feel	touch	smooth	solid	rough
grab	pressure	gritty	tight	uptight
pull	handle	pushy	soft	move
grasp	texture	sting	tough	thrust
rub	heavy	contact	sharp	tickle
sticky	firm	itchy	bounce	mime
get hold of	slip through	concrete	stumble	impression
get to grips	slimy	wobble	hit	dig
warm	catch	snag	dump	impact

Auditory-digital preferred system

These individuals will be talking to themselves about the logic, sense, rationality, of the information being provided. They want factual data with validating numbers and statistics. They consider the theoretical implications through logical analysis, and structured arguments. They make inferences, and project trends based on extrapolating the data under consideration. When communicating with the typical auditory-digital person, use *non-sensory* words, words that are 'neutral' with regard to any particular sensory system:

> "Will you find out, and let me know what you think about this? Go and explore this area, and consider the implications of what you discover, and provide me with a report that will increase my understanding."

Auditory-digital (neutral) words

basic	specific	understand	idea	learning
procedure	interesting	integrated	interactive	modular
tendency	obvious	incremental	balanced	virtual
knowledge	random	enhanced	variable	value-added
model	special	systematic	ecological	applications
theory	typical	optimal	boundary	flexibility
principle	usual	compatible	reciprocal	concept
meaning	excellent	paradigm	transitional	framework
know	think	contingency	experience	logical

If you are communicating with any of these types on a one-to-one basis, and you know or pick up what their preferred representational system is, you, by using the appropriate kind of *sensory* words will build rapport with them, and thus increase the probability of getting your message across. In NLP these sensory words are known as *predicates*. Some predicates will fall into more than one category, such as *light, soft, clear*; and others are multifunctional, such as *strong, fine, pattern*. People have different ways of coding sensory information, so they may not agree with you which category certain words are in. In that case, respect the other person's model of the world!

Matching Representational Systems in Groups

When training we recommend that you do your best to respect the four representational styles of learning, but there is no way you can possibly know anyone's particular preference. One way is to use 'neutral' words because they allow people to make sense of things in any way they like. For example, you can 'discover' things with your eyes, your ears, your hands, and with your senses of smell and taste. Because you are interpreting any non-sensory words in your preferred system – this respects your model of the world, and still maintains rapport with you, even though our understanding of 'discover' may be totally different.

The other way is to use all representational systems so that everyone in the audience will get their preferred system some of the time. And it will also help them to increase their flexibility in using their non-preferred systems. You are also helping them to match other people's preferences.

If you were to highlight only the visual system, then, on the face of it, it would look as though you were using mainly visual words. As an illustration: you would focus on your habitual system when you were under the spotlight in a stressful situation. Do you get the picture? People with a visual preference may indeed be seeing what we mean. But if you have a different preference you may be groping in the dark, because we are not on your wavelength, or we're making no sense at all. In a group, you will then lose those people who prefer to feel, or hear, or think conceptually.

If you use only one system while presenting or training, that would work fine, but only for about a fraction of the audience. What about the others?

- The auditory people would hear the message as sounding out of harmony. It doesn't chime with them.
- The kinesthetics can't quite grasp the thread, and feel that they are banging their heads against the wall, wondering how to demolish these communication blocks.
- And the auditory-digital people are analysing the content, ignoring the touchy-feely stuff, so they can concentrate on the basic parameters and logic of the thesis.

Increase your flexibility in communication by using words from every rep system. Then no matter what preference each person in the group has for learning and processing, they will be getting the information in the format that they want.

Does that make sense? Do you see what we mean? Does it sound like it is a good idea? Are you getting the hang of this? Or to summarise the essential elements of the foregoing theoretical explication, have you acquired a conceptual understanding of the pertinent factors that are involved in an appreciation of this mode of thinking?

Balancing styles
One of these representational systems will be easiest for you. But you should practice those representational systems that are not

easy or comfortable. This way you will find that you can balance your presentation and hit all the systems.

Exercise 19: Representational Systems

The next set of exercises is designed to give you practice and increase your flexibility in using the language of all systems.

Do this exercise in a group of five. It would make a good party game, because it is great fun to play. And this is playing, even though there is a serious intent. So take it lightly, and enjoy, because people learn much better when they are playful. Laughter is a good indicator!

You may find it useful to have the word lists for each of the rep systems in front of you, as prompts for words in your non-preferred systems.

This is what you do in your group of five:

- One person starts telling a story. Any story. Just make it up: "Once upon a time . . . " Tell two sentences of the story using *visual* words.
- After two sentences, the story passes to the next person, and they continue the story for two more sentences using *auditory* words.
- The next person adds two sentences using *kinesthetic* words.
- The fourth person uses *auditory-digital* words.
- And then back to *visual* words for the fifth person.
- Keep going around until everyone has told two lines of the story in each of the rep systems. Everyone has four turns in all.
- Notice how easy it is for you in each category.

Do this exercise with your group now.

Debrief

People usually find it is much easier using their preferred system, and they appreciate the word lists. The lists provide a good way of increasing your awareness of the language and your flexibility in using the different senses. Also, doing something outside of your familiar patterns of behaviour may seem uncomfortable, strange or artificial until you get used to it. Forcing you to use words from only one category pushes you to an extreme. When you then let that go again you will naturally drop back to using them all, without thinking about it. And it gets easier with practice.

Exercise 20: Incident – Point – Benefit and Rep Systems

Do this next exercise in your group. You are going to get up in front of your group, go into the trainer state, get connected, get rapport with your group, and then present your one minute incident – point – benefit four times, in each rep system.

This is what to do:

- Present your incident – point – benefit, predominantly in the *visual* rep system.
- Then present it again, predominantly using *auditory*.
- Then again, using *kinesthetic*.
- And finally, in *auditory-digital*.
- Notice what happens when you do that, both in yourself and in your group.
- And notice whether it makes it easier for you to do certain rep systems if you change your physiology or the things that you are doing inside yourself.

How to do this
Use the same story as before (or a new one that you can tell in four different ways, or even four different stories). This story will have some kind of representation in each system, even though you may not be aware of this yet. When you have your story, do the following:

- Concentrate on how you are representing this story to your-self on the inside.
- Notice which of the four rep systems you are using.

Now you are going to change the bias, so that you bring up one system to the maximum. Before you start talking, take a moment to rehearse your story.

- Think of it in pictures in your mind. Then illustrate what you can see to your audience in visual terms.
- Think of it in terms of how it sounds in your mind's ear, as you listen to all the noises being created in it. Then describe how it sounds to your audience using auditory words.
- Think of it in terms of the feelings: both the sensory experi-ence of the incident – any bodily feelings, touch, movement, temperature, and so on. Include your emotional responses to what is happening – the meaning you give to your internal sensations as a result of the sensory experience. Then use kinesthetic words to communicate these feelings across to your audience.
- Think of your incident – point – benefit in terms of the logic of the story, and the supporting factual, statistical or numeri-cal evidence, the argument, the pros and cons, and so on. Deliver this information as if you are presenting a business or technical report.

Do this exercise now, taking turns to tell your story in four different ways.

Debrief

Each time you tell the same story in a different rep system it takes on a new slant, and although it is the same basic story it will have a different effect on your audience. In a presentation or training, you wouldn't isolate one style; you would be using all systems combined for greater effect. By having a balanced mixture, you can accommodate everyone in the group.

Some topics lend themselves to one representational system over the others. On the one hand, for example, physical activities such as skiing, or mountain climbing, will be far easier to describe visually or kinesthetically. On the other hand, giving a financial report of last year's trading will probably be more challenging in visual, auditory, and kinesthetic, unless you can get to the experiences behind the data – what people were actually doing. Auditory-digital is an abstract level of description in which the sensory components have largely been filtered out. All you have to do is recover them, and then tell it like it is.

In general, auditory-digital is very easy to bring into business presentations or theoretical explanations. That's what those people want: "Give me the facts and figures. Give me the logic and rationality behind what we are doing." Then they will be satisfied. However, using this kind of abstract language will induce trance, and people will drift off . . .

Rep system practice
Here are some ways to practise using your non-preferred systems:

(All)   Choose one system to work with for the day. By concentrating on visual language, for example, you start noticing any visual words other people are using. Remember the filters we have for our experience: if you set up a filter for noticing visual predicates, then you will start noticing them. And you will be thinking visually, and also using visual predicates.

Choose a different filter each day. Next time you could filter for everything in the auditory system, and so on. And you can bring in Olfactory (smell) and Gustatory (taste) as well.

(V)   Sit for a while, indoors or outdoors, and use your visual sense to look around and count the number of different colours you see. Then start making finer discriminations by noticing the different shades and tints.

(A)   Sit down somewhere and count how many different sounds you can hear. If you are indoors, you may become aware of the sounds of voices, people moving about, equipment operating: computers, radios or music systems, clocks.

Then put your attention outdoors, and listen to the wind, the traffic, people passing by. As you simply count them, the more sounds you become aware of.

Organisational and cultural preferences
Our personal impression of organisational and cultural preferences, based on direct experience of different types of companies, is that there are definite variations in rep system preferences. For example, in computer companies or finance companies, we often find that 95% of the people have a preferred system of digital, and very few people using direct sensory systems. This seems to have some face validity, although we have no way of proving it statistically.

Now we don't know which way it works: whether having a preference for digital is why they chose that particular career, or whether doing that career shifted the balance. But if you are presenting or training in different organisational cultures they are likely to be skewed toward one particular system. Therefore you need to be flexible enough to work with all the representational systems.

The Communication Categories Model

Sometimes you want to communicate with a person on a one-to-one basis, and in order to match them, you need to know what their rep system preference is. Of course, you could talk in neutral language, or all systems, but it would be useful to know what that particular individual prefers.

Suppose someone in the group asks you a question, and you want to give them an answer which matches their preference, so that they will understand it, and get the most value from it. Now, apart from giving them a test, you need to have some other ways of finding out what their preferred rep system is. Sometimes it is appropriate in a training situation to give people tests, but in a business presentation, or even in everyday life, it is unlikely that you could get away with it.

There is a distinct physiology that goes with each rep system, which means there are other ways of finding out other people's preferences. Their preferred system actually affects the way they move, as well as the way they speak. It is also indicated by their body type, their posture and movements, the way that they breathe, the sound of their voice, and so on. So by becoming aware of their behaviour, noticing their physiology, and taking various other factors into account, you will assess an individual's preference. It also means that if you adopt the appropriate physiology yourself, you will find it easier to use that rep system.

Non-verbal communication comprises: our behaviour, the way we stand, the way we move, the gestures we use, our facial expressions, our voice tonality. All these will be communicating something to your audience. They are listed in the following table.

This table consists of generalisations, so there are probably exceptions to them; they are useful in that they seem to hold true in more than 50% of cases. So let's put some flesh on these bones.

The visual representational system
These people tend to have a straight posture, very upright, and very erect. They stand tall with their shoulders back, and their head up. Their body type will either tend to be very thin, very bony, and very angular – the extreme would be the marathon runner: long limbs, long bones, very thin, a very angular body type – or they will be the opposite of that and be obese.

They tend to move quickly, with tight, jerky, abrupt movements, and their eyes may be flicking from object to object. It is as if their eyes are leading them around and their body is trying to catch up with what they are focusing on.

Their breathing is shallow and high up in their chest. Because they are breathing high up, their voice will also originate high in their body, from their throat, upper chest, or even in their head. Try this for yourself. Imagine the origin of your voice is in your head, and notice its qualities when you speak. The pitch goes up, becomes clearer and a little louder.

Pattern	Visual	Kinesthetic	Auditory	Auditory-digital
Predicates which presuppose a rep system	See, look, vision, bright, focus, perspective, scan, colourful	Feel, grasp, touch, firm, warm, cool, get a handle on, get hold of	Hear, listen, loud, rings a bell, sounds like, harmonious, playing our tune	Statistically speaking, know, reasonable, logical, understand
Posture	Straight, upright, head and shoulders up	Curved, bowed, head and shoulders down	'Telephone' posture, head tilted to one side	Arms folded, erect, head up, one hand on chin
Body 'type' and movements	Either thin or obese; tight, jerky	Soft, full, rounded; loose, flowing	Inconsistent body; between loose and tight	Soft, full; rigid tension in neck and shoulders and jaw
Breathing	High up in the chest	Low in the abdomen right in the diaphragm	Full range, from high in chest to low in abdomen	Restricted, tight
Voice tonality, speed and volume	High, clear, fast and loud, coming from throat area	Low, airy, slow and soft, coming from abdomen	Melodic, rhythmic, variable, from throat to abdomen	Monotone, clipped, consistent
Eye elevation in relation to others	Above others looking up across the top	Below others looking down quite often to their right	Level, moving from side to side, often diverted down or away to listen	'Gazes' over others' heads, appears detached and dissociated

They tend to speak more quickly, because they see pictures in their head, and a picture paints a thousand words, but as they haven't got that much breath to describe it, they speak quickly to get everything out.

People accessing visually tend to look up. They are seeing pictures inside their head – remembering visually, or creating new pictures in their mind's eye. This elevation of the eyes may be happening momentarily, often out of awareness.

The kinesthetic representational system

Kinesthetic people tend to have a curved or bowed body, with their head and shoulders more down. There are two main types of body build: they either have a soft, full, or rounded physiology; or they have a very athletic build, the bodybuilder type, if they are into external kinesthetic, as in sports. They tend to have sort of looseness to their movements, and be quite flowing in the way that they move.

They breathe down in their *belly – diaphragmatic* breathing – and you will see some movement around the abdomen. Their voice tends to come from down there too, so it has a lower pitch. They have more breath to work with, so their voice often has an airy quality. They tend to speak more slowly, because feelings have more momentum and don't move as quickly as pictures. Someone accessing kinesthetically will look down to their right, and describe how they feel by speaking more slowly, using fewer words, and taking more time.

The auditory preferred system

Auditory people tend to have a more variable posture, more in-between. They may tend to tilt their head to one side, in the so-called telephone posture, as if they are holding a telephone to their ear. When you are speaking to auditory people, rather than look at you directly, they may turn their good ear to you, so that they can hear you clearly.

There is no generalisation in body type, and they will tend to be quite varied. Their breathing ranges from high up in their shoulders, to down in their belly, which means that their voice tonality also tends to vary considerably. The sound of their voice is quite important to them, and they will have a rich manner of speaking. When high auditory people speak to you it is almost like they are singing you a song. They are very melodic, and very rhythmical.

In terms of accessing information, with people who are processing auditorily, their eyes will be moving from side to side, looking to where their ears are.

The auditory-digital preferred system
Auditory-digital people commonly have their arms folded in front
of them, which tends to go with having an erect spine. In the original body language studies, the notion of someone having their
arms folded meant that they were blocking you out, and not interested. However, the auditory-digital person tends to sit there with
their arms folded when they are interested. So when you
encounter someone folding their arms you need to check out what
is going on for them. In itself that clue is unreliable. So you must
use other evidence to find out if they are interested in your ideas
and what you have to say.

Another typical physiology for auditory-digital is having one arm
crossed in front of the chest, with the other arm bent and the hand
on the chin – a variation of the Great Thinker pose. We will return
to this posture later when we consider Satir categories in Chapter
Thirteen.

Their bodies tend to be softer and fuller, but there is often a lot of
rigidity in the shoulder and neck area. So they might be experiencing some strain and stress around that particular area of their
body. They often have their jaw clenched, and if you look at the
area below their ears you will see their jaw muscles moving as
they grind their teeth, or talk to themselves inside their head.

Their breathing tends to be quite restricted because of this tension
in the neck. Just try this yourself for a moment:

● Tense up your shoulders, and then breathe.
   What effect does it have on your breathing?

Your breathing is restricted, because there is nowhere to expand
because of the muscle tension in the chest and shoulder area.

For them, voice tonality is irrelevant. The voice is just a means of
communication. All they are interested in is getting the facts
across to you: a data dump of pure information. The voice will
tend to have an even tonality – even a monotone.

When auditory-digital people are accessing memories and conversations, then, for all right-handed, and most left-handed people,

they will be looking down to their left. Sometimes when you are talking to an auditory-digital person, it will appear they have broken eye-contact with you, and are gazing through you, or over your head, and concentrating on something in the middle distance. This is their way of taking in what you are saying. So even though you may think, "This person isn't with me", they are. They are inside, processing the information you are giving them, and their eyes are simply 'disengaged', gazing at nothing in particular.

These are some general clues to noticing someone's preferred representational system, and to the way someone is processing at any particular moment. Noticing these will allow you to have an educated guess as to what someone's preferred representational system is when you first meet them.

So if you are finding there is one particular representational system that isn't easy for you to communicate in, then adopt the appropriate physiology. If visual is a challenge, then you will find it easier if you are upright and looking up. It is very difficult thinking visually while looking at the floor. But if you have a more erect posture, with your shoulders back, eyes up, and you are seeing pictures in your mind, then you will find it very easy to work with visual language, because that is the way it is coded into your physiology.

And now notice your state, how you are in yourself now, given that the last few pages of information have been pretty much auditory-digital information.

The Charisma Pattern

In the early days of NLP, researchers studied various presenters and speakers who were acknowledged as being highly charismatic. In particular: John F Kennedy and Martin Luther King. From this research emerged a common strategy that became known as the *charisma pattern*.

Charismatic speakers begin in kinesthetic: they start by speaking slowly in a low-pitched voice. There may be long pauses, almost hesitations in what they are saying. Sometimes they might be saying nothing at all to start with.

The general pattern is moving from kinesthetic through auditory to visual. And if you look at any of the films of any of those people, like Martin Luther King, or JFK, and if you pick out some other presenter, and you think to yourself, "Yes, that person is someone whom I would take as having charisma when they are in front of an audience", you will find that they do something like this:

Figure 11.1

$$K \rightarrow A \rightarrow V$$

So why would they be using this pattern? Think about the whole range of different preferred representational systems in the audience. If you want to get rapport with them all, you need to make sure you accommodate every preference.

If you started out in high visual, speaking very quickly, in a high-pitched voice, you would immediately get rapport with the visual people in the audience. However, you could blow rapport with the kinesthetic people, because their natural processing is far slower. They are working with feelings, and feelings have more momentum. So you would have a major mismatch.

The best thing to do is to pick up the kinesthetic people in the audience first, by matching with feelings. Once you have established rapport with these people, you then shift into auditory. You speed up a little, you vary your voice tonality a little more and raise the pitch of your voice, so that you are matching the auditory people. The kinesthetic people will come with you, because once you have rapport with someone, when you have matched them, you can then lead them somewhere else, and they willingly follow. So you lead them from kinesthetic into auditory, so they begin to process auditorily.

Now you pick up a third section of the audience. You match the auditory style for a while, get rapport with these people, and then you lead them all into the visual, by bringing your voice up higher in your body, speaking faster, using more visual words, and so on.

If you have done this correctly, you will find that you have brought all the kinesthetic and auditory people together with the visual people and everyone in the audience is now processing in the same way. Since everyone is processing in the same way, the whole audience is now with you. Everyone in the audience then thinks the person on stage has charisma, because everyone has been picked up, right from their preferred system of kinesthetic, through auditory, all the way to visual. And now everyone is with the presenter.

You can achieve this within the opening minutes of a presentation. If you watch any of those charismatic presenters in action, you will notice that by running through this pattern, they very quickly have everyone in the audience with them. They therefore generate that feeling which is one of synergy, of oneness, of being a group together. So we can add on the feeling that comes at the end of this sequence:

Figure 11.2

$$K \rightarrow A \rightarrow V \searrow$$
$$K$$

Once you have arrived at this point where everyone is together, you can then go anywhere you want, and they will come with you. You can take the whole audience on a rollercoaster ride through their representational systems: seeing things, feeling things, hearing things. In this way you will be bringing a great deal of variety into your audience's experience of you as a presenter or trainer.

What this means is that if you have people who normally process visually, and generally aren't in touch with their feelings, then you can enable them to feel certain things, which will enrich their experience. You could say that this is a way of bringing entertainment to your presentations and trainings. Not necessarily entertainment in terms of fun, humour, or interest, but entertainment as far as creating a rich sensory experience for your audience.

Use this at the beginning of your own presentations. Start by welcoming people in kinesthetic, using a lower-pitched voice, maybe being a little hesitant in the way you come across, by saying:

> "Good morning, how's . . . How is everyone doing? How are you feeling this morning? . . . So are you ready for this? Are you ready for, er, *Presenting Magically?*"

Then get slightly higher, faster, and less hesitant:

> "Well, hearing some of you talking outside while you were having coffee, it sounds like you are really excited about what we have to tell you over these three days."

Move into visual, so your voice is higher:

> "And if you take a look at the manual then you will see that in actual fact we have a great many new things to teach you, so that you can see how you can become such a magnificent presenter."

If you start out in kinesthetic right at the beginning of a training, the visual people, particularly high visual, may be thinking:

> "What on earth is this presenter doing? They're a bit fumbly, a bit slow, hesitant. Don't they know what they are doing?"

Fortunately they will quickly change their mind as soon as they detect they are being matched:

> "Oh, no, it's OK. They just started out slowly. They're OK now. I was a bit worried at first, but now I can see they're OK. It's looking good now they're moving at the kind of pace I like to see things at. Great."

This is an effective pattern that you may want to use in your own presentations. You might want to experiment with it in some of the exercises, and notice what happens. Anything that increases your rapport with the group is going to be useful.

Symmetry and Asymmetry

Another thing to think about, whether sitting or standing, is the notion of symmetry and asymmetry. The human body is more or less naturally symmetrical. That is, seen from the front or back, when the body in its resting state, each half of it is a mirror image of the other. As soon as we start to move, each half of the body will probably be doing different things.

We usually find that paintings, photographs, and illustrations are more pleasing to look at, more interesting to the eye, when the subject is asymmetrical: slightly to one side, or taken from an angle. Few portraits are taken straight on, unless they are being done for a special effect, or passport photographs. Many people claim to have their 'best side,' and the sitter will usually be arranged obliquely to the angle of view. Asymmetric views look more attractive than those straight on.

If you are sitting on stage and turn at an angle to the audience, then it is far more visually interesting. The audience gets an angled view of the presenter: they see a little bit of the front and a little bit of the side. That is particularly important when you are sitting down. You can explore this by watching people on the television. During the frequent occasions when the screen is filled with 'talking heads', turn the sound off, and notice the picture in terms of its composition, and especially the symmetry/asymmetry.

You can experiment, in your group, with different ways of sitting in front of the others, and what this feels like from the point of view of the audience. Try various orientations of the chair and your body on that chair. For example:

- Notice how having the chair at an angle is different from having everything square on to the audience. Which one do you think is more visually appealing?
- Notice how the energy changes, and the body-language 'messages' you are sending with the different postures.

Angular postures, and body-asymmetry have very different effects on the state of your audience. That is something else to be aware of when you are sitting down.

Chapter Twelve
Using Space

Spatial Anchoring

When you consistently do the same activity in the same place on the stage or area you are presenting from, then the people in the audience will make a connection between your position and that activity. For example, if you only tell stories and anecdotes when you are sitting down, that will mean that when you sit down, the audience knows what to expect: "Ah, time for a story."

This is another example of how we generalise our experience. Because this will be happening whether or not the people in the group are consciously aware of it, it means that you can create appropriate states in the group, so that they are ready for what is coming next, without having to tell them. Making a connection between a position on the stage and what you are doing is called *spatial anchoring* in NLP.

When training or presenting you can deliberately set up *anchors* with certain states in the audience. Sitting on a stool gives you one more thing you can use as an *anchor* or *trigger* for a certain state. For example, when seeking interaction with the audience, asking for questions, or comments about what they have discovered during an exercise, you can do it from downstage centre (DC). (We will use the theatre convention for describing these positions from the *presenter's* point of view (*Figure 12.1*). Down centre, for the audience, is at the front of the stage in the middle.) After a while, for that audience, asking questions and making comments will become associated with standing in that spot. As soon as you stand there, it means you want some interaction with the audience. And stand there *only* when you are talking with people in the group.

Figure 12.1

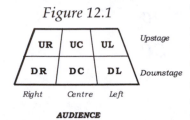

When you are ready to give some new information, just move to the right of the stage (DR), and give new information from only this place. After taking some questions, if you want to move onto the next thing, while finishing the last answer, just move back to (UR) and finish giving it from here. At an unconscious level, at least, that has already brought this interaction phase of the training to a close, and you are ready to move on.

Using specific parts of the stage for different aspects of your training or presentation is another way of beginning to control the state of your audience. After a while, just by moving from DC to UR and sitting down, people pick up their notebooks because they already know there is going to be some new information. If you just move randomly you are missing an opportunity to be able to instantly trigger expectations in the audience's mind, such as: "OK, now it is time to get some new information. Good."

Anchoring is about establishing expectations regarding the sort of things that might be happening. When you are planning your presentation or training:

- Decide how you are going to use these kinds of stage anchors.
- During the actual presentation, at first you may need to discipline yourself to be consistent, until it becomes habitual.

Voice anchors

You can also use a different voice tonality for different parts of the training. States easily get anchored or associated to certain tones of voice. And tying this in with your stage position, will strengthen the association. For example, by speaking hesitantly, with a lower pitch:

You can actually . . . shift the state . . . of an audience . . . just by . . . shifting the tonality . . . of your voice. If you set up certain . . . associations . . . as far as states are concerned . . . with certain . . . voice tonalities . . . you will notice . . . certain states . . . shifting . . . inside.

By contrast, by speaking faster and brightly: As soon as you change your voice tonality the state shifts again, because this is the voice you should normally use for giving new information.

Team presenting

Think about how you can use this material if you are presenting as part of a team. You need to know the particular skills that each of you possess, so that you can fully utilise them.

- The first person on stage should be the one who is best at getting rapport with a group, bringing the group together and getting them in a good state.
- In order to instantly transfer this rapport to the next person, you need to agree on certain words, a particular physiology, or a spot on the stage that you can associate with that particular state. When the next presenter comes on, they simply adopt the same physiology, the same voice tonality, stand in the same spot, and immediately they get the same rapport from the group without needing to build it up. It is like handing on the baton in a relay race; you need to be matching at each changeover.

This is what David did with that marketing director with the rotating hands gesture (Chapter Eight). Such a gesture was not one David would normally use, but since the marketing director had already established great rapport with the group, at the start of his presentation all David had to do was to stand in the same spot and use the same gesture while matching voice tonality. That way, David got rapport with the whole group straight away. This is a speedy way of building on the existing rapport.

If you are co-presenting with people who don't know a lot about these techniques, then you need to teach them. We would suggest you always teach them some basics around rapport, and positive internal representations, to ensure they are communicating what you want to get across.

Until your co-presenters are proficient, take responsibility yourself for building rapport with the group. Then as soon as you know you have it, you can transfer it to your colleague by shifting your physiology so that it is the same as theirs. That would instantly put this person in rapport with the group, even though they hadn't done anything themselves.

Now what do you do if the presenter before you has not done very well, and as a result the audience is not in a good state? In this instance, the most important thing is what you don't do. If you come onstage and take up the same position and posture, the audience will transfer whatever state they are in onto you, and you will get that same response. Then you are going to have to work hard to dig yourself out of that. Therefore:

- Adopt a completely different posture, stand somewhere else on the stage, and use different gestures. Then you can start afresh.

Taking words back

If you are ever on stage, or presenting to a group, and you judge from the response in the audience that you just said something that was the wrong thing to say – and you will know that from the audience's response – and you think, "Oh no! I can't believe I said that! I wish I could take those words back", with that kind of experience – and even seasoned presenters have them – you can 'mismatch yourself'. You can't actually take the words back, but there is a way around it. Here is what to do:

- Take a step to the side, like you are stepping out of your body.
- From this apart position, indicate the place where you were standing when you said the wrong thing, and say, in amazement: "Can you believe he said that? I'd never say anything like that. Whew!"
- Then carry on, still standing in this new position.

The audience will then have the memory that those words came out of someone else's mouth, not yours. Those words will probably not be linked with you at all.

If once you have said the wrong thing, you stay in the same place, anything more that you do in that position, such as trying to justify or explain it away, will just be digging yourself in deeper. So immediately, actually step away from it, change your physiology. Remember the relative importance of different parts of the communication: the words count for less than your physiology. The message is that you are dissociating from something you do not want to be attached to, and because you are in rapport, the audience will do the same.

Dealing with a lectern
Many organisers think that a lectern is a useful adjunct to any presentation. For many presenters the lectern is something they grip, white-knuckled, for support, to prevent them from collapsing on the floor!

With modern technology, you can now have a lectern with a head-up screen, connected to a computer, that will display your script. You can look straight ahead at the glass screen and it seems as though you are looking at the audience and you know your words. In fact you are simply reading them. Such a device may seem tempting. But it can also lock you into a rigid performance. Where ever possible avoid reading off a script. When you have developed these *Presenting Magically* skills, such gadgetry merely gets in your way, and prevents you from giving of your best.

Whenever you encounter any kind of lectern, if possible, ignore it. At least the reason for not standing behind a lectern is that it has become an anchor for all those presenters before you, and has a wealth of accumulated associations, mostly undesirable. Just by picking up the lectern and moving it to one side, you break the pattern of associations. If it won't move, do your presentation from in front of it.

A lectern creates a physical barrier between you and the audience. You want to be able to move around and use the whole stage. Although energy operates regardless of any physical barriers – you can still send energy out there, and be aware of the energy in the room – the energy sending/receiving process is hindered by this visual block between you and the audience.

You must find out about any such constraints when you are negotiating your contract for the presentation, and deal with these matters ahead of time. For example, if the lectern or your position is fixed because of microphones or television cameras, then you will need to clarify how you will be wired up, and how much movement you can make. Organisers have said to us:

> "I'm sorry, but with the sound system that we have got, you are going to have to be behind the lectern."
> "Either you get us mikes, or we'll shout."

That produces results! We prefer a radio mike because it allows you to roam freely, without tripping over wires.

Be especially wary if there will be other people sitting on stage while you are presenting. In our culture, where we read from left to right, there is a natural tendency for the eyes to be scanning across the stage from left to right. Generally speaking, in theatrical terms, stage right (DR) is a weak position if there are other people on stage, because all eyes will be scanning across and looking at everyone other than you. If they are seated further back, they will very easily be *upstaging* you. Just making small movements will be distracting. Therefore it is better to stand stage left (DL), or, if you must, arrange for the lectern to be there, as this will give you a stronger, more powerful position and you will have more of the audience's attention.

Changing the audience's state

If there is no way of getting around any constraints, then dramatically shift the audience's state, and get them re-anchored to you. So if you follow a presenter who has created a rather down state in the audience, a slightly risky strategy would be to say something like, "Well, I don't know about you, but I think it is time to do something different!" It would probably get a welcome response. But be careful what you say. It is neither a good idea, nor ethical, to pour scorn on other presenters, especially if you ever want to present there again.

To change the audience's state you could crack a joke, get them laughing – at your expense, rather than at someone else – and thus get the laughter associated to you. That will immediately change the energy level. Or you could introduce a physiological change in the audience. Anthony (Tony) Robbins, a very famous motivational speaker, does this at the beginning of many of his presentations. He will say:

> "You have all been sitting here for quite some time. And I know it is quite warm in the room. So let's all just stand up for a second."

He gets the whole group standing up. Then he will say:

> "So everyone stretch over to your left . . . "

and he will get the audience doing these stretching exercises.

Standing up means you change your physiology and thus your state. But what else has he done? He has established rapport, because he got everyone in the audience doing the same thing as he is. He has also taken control of the group, by saying, "OK, everyone stand up". He stands there and does nothing until everyone stands up. He has given a series of commands, "Do this", and they have done it. So Tony has control of the group, he has rapport with the group, and he has also shifted their state. Now he can present. And he does this before he begins presenting every single time, whether he is starting a training, or coming on as the second speaker.

Owning the stage
When you are doing any kind of presentation, it is important that you have a sense of 'owning the stage'. Whether you are the first or the tenth presenter on, when you get there in front of the audience, you have to own the stage. You have to convey to them: "This is my place. I am at home here. I own it." It helps ownership to have made sure you have the stage set up exactly the way you want it. So when you walk on stage, physically pick up a lectern, put it over on the side, walk back to the centre, and then start off, you have conveyed unconsciously to everyone in the group, "I am in control. I am going to create the space that I want, in order to be who I want to be. If I am behind a lectern, I'm not going to be in

the state I want to be in". You might say: "OK. Do you want me to speak here or not?" Having it the way you want it is important, because when you have that, you can then own the space.

Before the audience arrives at your presentation take the time to get comfortably familiar with the stage, and the surroundings, so that you can be 'at home' there. 'Walk the boards'. notice where everything is, both on stage and in the auditorium. Sit in the auditorium, stand at the back, so you know what the audience will see. Notice any 'dead' spots, and find where the most powerful spot on the stage is. Even before you start, stand where you are going to be presenting on the stage, and fill all the space with your energy, of the appropriate quality. Expand your energy field to fill the entire space, so that it is part of you.

Tad recalls, "Our major learning in this came from a training we do in Hawaii. We start with an ancient Hawaiian hula ceremony, and some of the hula dance performers are just four or five years old, and many of them are in competition. There was one little girl, about five, who was technically perfect at the hula, but she had been getting only second or third place in the international hula contests. So I spoke to her hula teacher and said, 'There is only one thing she needs to do. And then she will win every single competition she enters. She is technically brilliant, but the only thing she isn't doing yet is owning the stage. She is there, doing it perfectly, but the space isn't hers.'"

The next time we saw this girl dance, about three months later, she came on and owned the stage. As she walked on her whole presence gave out the message, "This is my stage. You are going to watch me. I deserve all of your attention". And she got it. You could sense the energy shift in the audience instantly. Since then she won her hula competition and a number of others as well – because she now owns the stage.

Using flipcharts
Many presenters use a flipchart for writing up significant points. In our trainings, we have the flipchart stage right, which means it is on the audience's left, and usually slightly raised up for them. Here is the reason for that: For most people in the audience, looking

up and to their left will put them into *visual remembered* mode. This is another generalisation.

Try this with a partner. Say to the other person:

- "See again the house where you lived when you were a child."
- "See again your favourite toy."
- "See again your schoolroom." And so on.

You are instructing them to access particular memories. As you give this instruction watch what they do with their eyes. It happens quite quickly, so you need to be observing while you give the instruction. Use the words, "See again . . . " because you are giving a command. If you say, "Can you see . . . ?" they may be going into internal dialogue as they discuss the possibility with themselves!

Although people's eyes are moving all the time, when they access visual memories they will commonly briefly look up and to the left. (Some left-handed people have this reversed.) This phenomenon has been systematically explored only since the beginning of NLP.

Therefore rather than having the flipchart up centre, we put it over on the audience's left (UR), and having people looking up at it, as it is on a raised stage. The same thing applies using a computer based system, such as Microsoft PowerPoint™. Position the screen in accordance with the preferred system of accessing *visual remembered* for most people. As we are matching how their brains have coded the process of accessing visual memories, it will help them in remembering the pictures, diagrams, or words that we put on the flipchart. We put all the flipchart pages around the room for the remainder of the training, so that the information written on them will stay in the audience's peripheral vision to be continually absorbed. These flipcharts become anchors, so that just catching sight of them from time to time assists people in remembering all the material we have been talking about. For example, glimpsing the brief summary overleaf (*Figure 12.2*) brings back the information about the charisma pattern. So if you are thinking, "What did David say about the charisma pattern?"

by looking at the diagram, you would probably find that it allows you to access all the details.

Figure 12.2

$$K \rightarrow A \rightarrow V$$

Using OHPs
If you are using the overhead projector (OHP), is it better to reveal the information all at once, or to cover part of it, and reveal it stage by stage? – We no longer use OHPs at all. We use Power Point™, which means you can put the bullet points up separately, one at a time. If you must use OHPs, put only one point per slide.

The important thing about using flipcharts or OHP slides is that you put on the flipchart or slide only what you want the audience to remember. For example, the charisma pattern structure in *Figure 12.2*, is about as much as we would ever put on a slide or a flipchart. No more than that, because what is on the slide is just a visual trigger or reminder for the information, rather than conveying the information itself. If you want the audience to have vast quantities of facts and figures, give them printed handouts.

Dealing with ephemeral information
There will be times when you are drawing out or collecting information which you need to have in front of you before you decide what to do with it. Now, you might not necessarily want the audience to remember the information. You are just using it in order to move on to the next stage. Suppose, for example, a problem has arisen for the group. As they tell you about the current problem situation, write the details on the flipchart. Then tear off this 'problem sheet' and put it up on the wall. Next, start working on possible solutions, and write these on a new flipchart. This is what you want them to remember. The problem is now associated with the sheet on the wall, and the solutions are associated with the flipchart. Then, you can reach over and take the problem sheet off the wall, and throw it in the trash bin. Metaphorically you are saying: "We have handled the problem. Let's focus on the solution."

Remember that everything you do communicates something. Everything. Even if your audience is not consciously aware of what you are communicating – you are still communicating to them. They will be aware of the fact that you have just wadded up the problem and put it in the trash, and that will have some key associations for them, at some level of awareness.

Chapter Thirteen
Non-Verbal Communication

Have you ever encountered presenters with extremely distracting styles? They pace up and down, exhibit nervous tics, jingle coins in their pocket, use weird gestures. Maybe they have an unusual way of speaking that is hard to understand, or drives you crazy. If so, you were probably not paying attention to the *content* of what they were saying, and you ended up with a confused or garbled version of their talk. If your tonality or body language does not support the content of your presentation, then your message is unlikely to be heard.

Non-Verbal Patterns of Communication

When first presenting and training, people often wonder what to do with their hands. Hands seemed to have a life of their own, and were distracting to us, as well as the audience. Do we put them in our pockets; hold them rigidly down by our sides; hide them behind our backs, clutching a board marker; or do we clasp them modestly in front in the 'figleaf' posture?

We found the answers by studying the Satir category patterns. These five non-verbal patterns of communication are specific postures and gestures that involve your entire body, including your hands. Each has an accompanying voice tonality. These distinctions come from Virginia Satir – one of the models of excellence studied by the originators of NLP. She was a family therapist who developed an effective ways of working with whole families together. She described four dysfunctional ways in which people communicated. The fifth one, the Leveler, was added later.

Each category seems to have cultural associations, so adopting one particular physiology will trigger not only a certain state within you, it will also create a certain state within your audience. They are international; they work across cultures. We know this because we train people, including NLP trainers, from all over the world. Since learning these Satir categories, they report that using the categories works very successfully in their own countries.

Here is a brief summary of these non-verbal communication patterns.

Non-verbal patterns of communication

Leveler   Symmetrical physiology: upright, moving hands, palms down, in a downward movement and spreading
"This is the way it is", "This is true."

Placater   Symmetrical open physiology, palms up, moving in an upward direction
"Help me", "I'm open", "I want to please you."

Blamer   Asymmetrical: leaning forward, and pointing the finger
"It's your fault", "It's down to you."

Computer   Asymmetrical: hand on chin or arms folded, 'thinker' pose, academic lecturer stance
"I'm the authority", "I'm reasonable, logical and sensible", "Here are the the facts."

Distracter   Asymmetrical physiology: angular, disjointed and incongruent
"I don't know", "It's not my fault."

In the following examples we will indicate which role we are adopting with a bracketed label, such as (Leveler) or (Distracter). You will have to imagine the accompanying posture, gestures, hearing the tonality shifts as we change roles, sometimes very quickly within one sentence.

Leveler

We have already briefly covered Leveler in Chapter Seven. It is that balanced posture you were adopting while exploring the trainer state. Your weight is evenly balanced, your hands are palm down and flat, and symmetrically moving from mid-chest downwards and outwards. With Leveler your voice has a falling tonality, and you are slowing down as you do the movement.

Generally Leveler asserts authority and calms people down, so it is very good for bringing things down to earth. When people see that movement and hear that tonality it is as though they are getting the message: "Let me give you the facts. Believe me. This is how things are around here."

When using Leveler, pause at the end of the statement.

(Leveler)   "So let me tell you the point of this." *(Pause)*.

That opens up the space. They know there is something important about to come. They know they are going to get some factual information, about the way things are. So you pause . . . *(speaking slowly and deeply)*:

(Leveler)   "This is the point. *(Pause)* Using this physiology in your presentation will transform your stage presence. *(Pause)*. Totally."

Using a falling tonality and pauses makes a big difference.

Placater

Placater has palms upward, in an open gesture, with the hands moving upward, often with a slight bow of the head *(Figure 13.1)*. Compare this gesture with Leveler: notice the shift that happens when the palms are up. Notice the difference in your state with this posture. Placater suggests openness, vulnerability. Placater agrees with everything, talks in an ingratiating way, and is always trying to please. They generally have very little self-esteem, and they live their lives through approval from others:

"I'm listening. And I agree."
"I'm sorry. I'm only trying to please you."

In the full version of Placater you would actually go down on one knee, in a supplicating gesture, with both hands up, one higher than the other, asking:

"Please help me. I want to do the right thing. I want to please you, so tell me what I must do, so that you will be OK."

Figure 13.1

Blamer

Blamer is accusing someone. They lean forward, with arm raised, pointing a finger of blame (*Figure 13.2*). They are inquisitorial, although they are not interested in getting answers. Blamer comes from a position of superiority and is more interested in throwing his/her weight around, making others wrong:

Figure 13.2

"Why are you so (x)? You never do anything right. What's the matter with you?"

"I'm the boss around here. What I say goes. Get it?"

It is unlikely that you would use the full Blamer posture when presenting. You wouldn't point at a particular person, because that might trigger stuff around being told off at school, or some similarly unpleasant kind of thing. You don't necessarily use Blamer with "I'm blaming you", or to communicate to someone that they are at fault in any way. Remember that you are directing energy with your finger, so take care, and soften it slightly, and point above the heads of the group. Rather than use one finger, use two fingers together, or your fingers shaped like a beak, as this is less confrontational.

Blamer brings life to the presentation by raising the energy. Use Blamer physiology to push the point home, to literally punch the key points of your message:

> "There are *three* points I want you to get. The *first* point is . . . ; the *second* is . . . "

You are adding emphasis, indicating what matters, while telling your audience that it concerns them.

One effective, but somewhat unusual use of Blamer is to use it to empower an individual. (Pointing at the individual), "You can do it!"

Computer

Computer is more thoughtful and passive, very reasonable, with no feelings showing. Computer has one arm across the chest, and the other hand on the chin in a thinking posture (*Figure 13.3*). Computer's voice is monotonous, their words are likely to be abstract. One version of this would be the auditory-digital person. For example:

> "Well, it seems that this situation necessitates someone here exhibiting a modicum of rationality. So I have presumptuously taken it upon myself to represent all that is logical, rational and reasonable."
> "It would appear reasonable that if one were to adopt certain physiologies, then the concomitant would be that it would engender certain responses within an audience. Because statistically, these physiological positions would logically tend to suggest certain characteristics of the presenter."

The Computer is the pedagogue, the college professor, the dispassionate scientist – cool, calm, and collected:

Figure 13.3

(Computer) "I'm being completely rational and analytical about this. It therefore falls upon me to explain to you how this all makes logical sense."

Use Computer in situations where you want to communicate: "I'm thoughtful, I'm thinking about what you said … " Go into Computer if someone asks you a question, and you need to buy some time to answer it: "Mm. Let me think about that for a moment." You are honouring their question by thinking about it, in order to give them a great answer.

Figure 13.4

Distracter

Distracter is total asymmetry, with a very angular spine and the arms at different angles and at different heights *(Figure 13.4)*. You could think of your body as going off in several different directions at once. In fact, any asymmetrical posture is distracting. With it goes a fluctuating voice, which is distracting because it is unpredictable: high then low; fast then slow. Sometimes it is breathy, charming, wheedling, a 'little girl' voice of no substance – the scatterbrain, bimbo, or babe; with men, the 'little boy lost' or the wimp. At other times the voice is deep, and sincere, or even jokey. It is often just words for words' sake – meaning is irrelevant. You never quite know where you are; nothing the Distracter says is to the point.

Remember the exercises where you were moving your energy centre around your body. To do Distracter, you need to have your centre constantly on the move, and actually going outside of your physical body at times, such as orbiting around your head. This will make you dizzy, so you keep moving, trying to maintain your balance, and failing.

One common gesture would be the 'teapot': one arm is up and pointing out, the other down and pointing in, the head twisted to one side, the shoulders uneven. Some students call it the "Don't shoot the trainer" posture.

(Distracter) "Well, you know, don't blame me, it's nothing to do with me. I'm just the trainer, you know."

This posture can be very useful for distracting hecklers. If someone were heckling you, they would be using Blamer. Blamer is totally deflected by Distracter – the accusations just bounce off. So if a heckler starts with:

(Blamer) "Well, I don't agree with you as far as this is concerned,"

and you respond:

(Distracter) "Well, I mean, what do you want me to do about it? You know."

Shrug and shake your head, and you will totally diffuse the Blamer's energy.

You can also diffuse all the energy from the heckler's Blamer posture by going into the Distracter posture, opening your eyes wide, and saying:

(Distracter) "Well, I don't know . . . "

or "Oh, really?"

The rest of the group will almost always laugh at that, which will keep them on your side, rather than on the heckler's.

Exercise 21: Satir Categories

In your group, try out each of these Satir categories for yourself:

- Adopt the posture, add the gestures, and say some of the typical sentences using the relevant tonality. Notice the change in your state as you do it.
- Have someone else do each category in front of you, so that you become familiar with being on the receiving end, hearing that voice tonality and seeing that physiology.

Now, do this experimenting in only your group, rather than the people you spend most of your life with. Husbands, wives, boyfriends and girlfriends, work colleagues, and so on, are not the appropriate people for you to check out responses to these Satir categories because there could be other things going on, other anchors already set up with particular postures.

Do this exercise now.

Putting them together . . .

(Computer) Does that begin to make comprehensible how you might possibly utilise specific postures to achieve certain outcomes within a group? By implementing them in combination, the underlying rational considerations become apparent.

(Blamer) And I will tell every single one of you now, when you use these Satir categories, as they are called in NLP . . .

(Leveler) . . . it will totally transform your presentation.

(Placater) Now, help me out here. Do your best in the exercises, because I really want you to succeed at it, you know. I really do.

(Blamer) And if you don't get the result that you want, it's up to you to just do it again, because you already know . . .

(Leveler) . . . there is no such thing as failure – only feedback.

See how they fit together?

(Leveler)   It gives you something to do with your hands.

(Computer) And instantly enables you to control the state of the audience, moment by moment, just by engaging in a few archetypal postures, during the ongoing presentation situation.

(Distracter) And it's fun too. Hey. Bit of a laugh. Great!

(Placater)   So please give it a try. I'm sure you'll like it. Really.

Practise using them all, relating them to what you are doing in a particular presentation. In the exercises, you will probably find that you have a preference for one of these physiologies, and therefore tend to use it most of the time. So if Placater is your favourite, you will tend to present with that posture all the time, which may be indicating some sort of openness but also hinting that you are insecure and need assurance. If you are using Placater all the time in a business or a sales presentation, it probably won't be giving you enough power in your message. It would be better to say:

(Leveler)   "Let me tell you what we can do for your business."

With Leveler you are bringing the energy down and smoothing it out. This is very different from the jagged energy of Distracter, which is all over the place:

(Distracter) "Well, I'm just a bit . . . You know. What did you say?"

Compare this with:

(Leveler)   "We can do this for your business. I think that if you hire us as a training company then we can improve your profits. Honestly. Many of our clients have said that they can't believe the amount of benefit they gained from our doing a training for them."

Distracter is miles away:

(Distracter) "Really?"

Placater pleads:

(Placater) "So what do you think? Do you want to hire us?"

Blamer does not beat about the bush:

(Blamer) "Do you want this or not?"

These are all very different. They all affect the energy, and they all will be appropriate in particular circumstances.

Sitting down
You can adapt all of the categories so that they work when you are sitting down. Remember that when you are seated the energy drops, and there is a tendency for things to get a little heavy, more serious. Sitting down, by itself, is rather like leveling: it brings the energy down. Therefore when you are seated use Distracter to counterbalance the leveling effect, and raise the energy up, and use Blamer to keep the energy out. Use the gestures at head height. Your voice will take on a higher pitch, and will be coming from higher in your chest. It is sometimes easier to keep the energy moving, by using your arms more, and doing Distracter horizontally, with your hands more or less level, but at varying distances from your body, your arms bent in different ways, remaining wide-eyed. This sitting-down variation of Distracter will raise the energy, make it lighter and more fun.

Although you can adapt the Satir categories for sitting down, in a sales presentation it is far more effective to stay standing up, because you need to have more control of your energy. Standing up also makes these non-verbal parts of the communication easier to use.

Make sure that what you are doing is appropriate for the context. If, for example, you are confirming an appointment with a company to do a training day, then using Distracter is going to come across as incongruous. So use Leveler there, because you are dealing with the facts and getting them clear.

Exercise 22: Using Satir Categories

In this exercise you can combine the five Satir categories with your incident – point – benefit stories. This is what you do:

- Go into the trainer state, connect with your group, and so on.
- Do your incident – point – benefit story again. By this time you should know your stories so well that you can concentrate on the Satir categories. As you do your incident – point – benefit, spend at least 30 seconds, and preferably the full minute, in each one of the Satir categories. For example, do the whole incident – point – benefit in Leveler, and notice what happens.
- Then do the whole thing in Placater, in Computer, in Blamer, and finally in Distracter.
- Notice what happens in your own state, as you go into the different physiologies.
- When you are in the audience, notice the different states that you go into when you hear these stories in the different ways.
- Alternatively, you may choose to do your one minute incident – point – benefit with the first half in Leveler, and the second half of it in, say, Placater.
- Finally, do your incident – point – benefit using all five categories as you tell it. Just trust yourself to use the appropriate Satir category for the emphasis that you want to make at that particular point. Play with this to find out what happens.
- Notice which particular Satir category works best with the incident – point – benefit. Notice also how it brings your whole presentation to life and enables you to convey the message more fully, because you are bringing in the physiology as well.

Do this exercise now in your group before reading on.

Debrief

People will be picking up meaning from this non-verbal communication all the time, and may even be getting more from it than from the story itself. The body language you use is a really important part of your telling of the story. Now that you are using this 55% segment of your communication to enhance the 7% verbal content, you will find you are communicating far more effectively. Using the Satir categories will completely transform your presentation.

When you were the presenter in the exercise, did you notice how your state changed as you went into each category? As soon as you go into Leveler, your energy shifts, and your state changes. When you are in rapport with a group, going into Leveler will change the audience's state as well. Then, maintaining rapport, you can lead them into different states.

You will soon discover which particular Satir category you habitually tend to use. It is the one you do most easily. So don't work on that one; work on the others. If Distracter is your preferred mode, then concentrate on doing Leveler, which is its opposite. You can stretch yourself and do your next presentation all in Leveler. In that way it really becomes ingrained in your neurology.

Women in the business environment

There is one particular thing with women and Leveler. We are still unfortunately in the situation where many business environments are very male-oriented. So as a businesswoman going in to do a presentation, you may well find that the audience is predominantly male. Many men in the business environment still have to deal with traditional stereotypes as far as women in business are concerned. Putting those stereotypes in terms of the Satir categories, women are seen as either Distracters or Placaters.

This is how you turn the whole thing around. As a woman going into a predominantly male business environment, start your presentation in Leveler:

(Leveler)   "OK, now let me tell you what we can do for your business."

When women do that, you get an immediate shift in the men present: "Whoa! Hang on a minute!" It has upset their expectations. As a woman doing Leveler you have completely blown the stereotypes and generalisations that many men have around how women behave, and they can no longer fit them on you. Now you are starting from a clean sheet – which is very powerful. So, if you are a woman presenter in a business environment – it is different in other contexts – and you have a predominantly male audience, use a lot of Leveler, as it will completely transform the response you get.

Talking in quotes

You can use Blamer *in quotes*, which means that you actually say the words, but they are attributed to someone else. For example:

> This person said to me (*Blamer*), "You had better take responsibility for using these things, because if you don't use them, you won't get the results". Now I wouldn't actually say anything like that. But this person did. And they may have a point.

When you embed the message in another one, you completely dissociate the listeners away from yourself, but the words have still gone in. And while you have punched them in with Blamer, it is not actually you that is doing the blaming, and you are not blaming anyone in particular. However, the effect is there.

Inflexion patterns

Now let's look at that 35% sector of the pie chart – the tonality of how you say things, the inflexion patterns in the sentences you use, and, in particular, the three structures that separate communications into statements, commands, and questions.

With Distracter, people tend to go up at the end of a sentence. In the following examples this rising inflexion at the end of a phrase or sentence will be indicated by using *italics*. Then every sentence sounds like a *question*. So for example:

(Distracter) "I am not really *sure* about what I am *saying*. And because I am *uncertain*, you can't really blame me for *anything* that I am *doing*, because it is not my *fault*. Because I am not really *responsible*. I'm just the *trainer* here, you *know*."

If, at the end of each phrase, you have a rising inflexion on the last word you say, that will definitely have an effect on your audience.

Voice intonation patterns
These voice inflexion patterns can be represented graphically as in *Figure 13.5*. Each W represents a word or phrase in a sentence, and the lines indicate the inflexion pattern: level, rising or falling. If the lines are all horizontal, you are making a statement. If the line goes up at the end, you have a question; and if it goes down, it is a command.

Figure 13.5

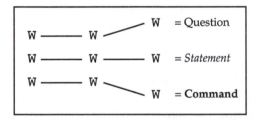

Questions
On the top line of *Figure 13.5*, if your voice tonality in a sentence is, "Word, word, word", it will sound like a question. Its tonality unconsciously communicates, "I am asking you a question". *(Rises in tonality are indicated by italic text.)*

There are people who go up at the end of every *sentence*. Although you are actually making a *statement*, it sounds as though you are asking a *question*, or you are not really *sure* about what you are *saying*.

Statements

If your voice tonality stays level throughout the whole sentence, then that suggests to the unconscious mind that you are making a statement. The middle line represents the tonality which indicates a statement:

"Here is a statement. And it is on the level."

Commands

If your voice tonality goes down at the end of a sentence, as on the bottom line, that is unconsciously taken as a command. *(Falls in tonality are indicated by **bold** text.)*

"Make this sentence a **command**. This is what you do."

Even if you ask someone a question, but you go down in voice tonality at the end of the question, the unconscious mind will take it as a command.

"So do you want to hire our **company**?"
"Do you want to register for the **training**?"

You have asked a question, but unconsciously it is taken as a command.

Confirming the appointment

For example, one of our students was the general manager of a company that supplied drinks to vending machines. He had a telesales team making appointments for his salespeople to visit other companies. The salesperson would turn up at the appointed time, demonstrate their products, and hopefully get the contract. However, what he found was that only 54% of these appointments actually took place. Roughly half the time the salesperson would arrive at a particular client's site and find that their representative was either busy, or away doing something else. This was wasting the salespeople's time.

So the manager sat in with his telesales team to observe exactly how they were making appointments. He had already taught them the basics of rapport building. But one of the key things he noticed was that when the telesales person was confirming the appointment, they were using the questioning tonality. They would say:

(Question) "Let me just *check*. So you have agreed to see our sales person. So our *salesperson* will be there on *Wednesday,* at four-*thirty."*

They were restating what had been agreed; the actual content of the statement is OK. But they were using a final rising inflexion – the questioning tonality – which led the listener to think it was either a question, or in doubt. So he taught his telephone sales people to use the command tonality when they were confirming the appointment. So now they would say:

(Command)"You have agreed to see our representative on **Wednesday**. At 4.30 pm. Is that **OK**?"

This is different. The manager noticed an immediate change. Having taught his telesales team about rapport, and which inflex-ion pattern to use when confirming an appointment, the number of appointments taking place went up to 92%, compared with 54% before, which meant his salespeople were in front of their prospective clients far more of the time. The *total* number of appointments the salespeople were making stayed roughly the same, but now nearly all booked appointments took place. Even though the salespeople's performance stayed constant, they were now visiting almost twice as many clients, and consequently there was a proportional increase in business.

Use the command tonality to define what you want to happen, for example, when making an appointment, confirming a contract, or closing a sale. In presentations and trainings use these different tonality patterns to get answers – or not. There will be times when you want people to ask you questions, and other times when you want to move on. There are also times when you want to make it appear to the audience that they are free to ask questions if they want to, but you don't really want them to.

When you want questions, comments or audience participation, this is what you do:

- Ask a question with a *questioning* voice tonality
- Raise your eyebrows at the end of the question, and keep them raised until you get a response.

When someone in the audience picks up the questioning tonality, the raised eyebrows, they get a sense of expectation. Keep your eyebrows raised until someone says something. They will very likely want to oblige you, so you won't have to wait long.

Sometimes you might not want any questions because of time constraints, or it is just before an exercise and you want the group to get on with it and have the experience, rather than explore all their *what ifs*.

Other cultures

In several other cultures and language groups, people use different patterns. For example, in the speech patterns of Australia and Canada there is a tendency to go up at the end of sentences. The same thing applies to Dutch, and probably many other languages. We have done a lot of training in Holland, and when we point out that they are using the questioning tonality when making statements, they tell us that it does create doubt for them. So, generally speaking these intonation patterns hold true. The Dutch and the Australians tell us that the rising inflexion at the end of a sentence is OK when they are in their own culture. But even when they are in their own culture, switching to this command tonality gives them even more impact.

If you are wondering about the best way of handling these differences when working with people from different cultures, then you probably don't need to do anything different. For example, in Holland, when we use embedded commands – which we are doing throughout our trainings – using the command tonality still works.

Having the distinctions in place
The important thing about this – and this is true of all of NLP – is that people are doing these things anyway, and all it takes is for you to have the appropriate filters in place so that you can recognise when it is happening. Once you understand the pattern, you can use it to your advantage in the appropriate context.

When you are discerning what people are doing, it is not the case that they do it once and if you blink you'll miss it. People are very consistent, and their programming means they do things over and over again. Be patient, and you will see and hear these repeating patterns.

Start by modeling those people who are really good at something. From what you are learning here, you now know some of the things worth modeling. For example, you can now recognise, "They use a lot of Leveler", or, "They are using command tonality", and so on. Once you have some fundamental distinctions in place, you will easily notice what others are doing.

So if there are particular presenters of whom you think: "Wow, that person is a really good presenter/trainer", then get them on video, or at least some audiotapes of them doing their stuff, take what you are learning in this book, and model what they are doing.

At the end of the day, as far as all of this material is concerned, the most important consideration is not whether something is true or not. It doesn't matter whether something is true. What matters is:

- Does it work?
- Does this give me the results I want?

If you are ever in doubt about what to do, then remember the attitudes of curiosity and wanton experimentation. You now have the ability to try out different ways of being with other people, and the sensory acuity to notice what is working. If you start wondering, "What is the best thing to do here?" then get curious, do them all, and find out which way of doing things delivers the best results.

Chapter Fourteen
The 4MAT System

Here's a system that formats your presentation and makes it understandable to the broadest percentage of the population.

The 4MAT System comes from a study of learning styles by Bernice McCarthy. She noticed that when she was teaching children in school, they learned in different ways. In particular, they learned by asking specific questions. She put the children into four basic categories, according to their particular mindset, as follows.

- Some children wanted reasons. They were habitually asking the question *Why?*:
  "Why are we doing this? Why does this happen . . . ?"
- Others wanted facts. They would be asking for information, the *What?*:
  "Tell me about that. How many different sorts are there? What are they called? Where do they come from? What do they do?"
- Others would be very pragmatic. They wanted to do things, to find out *how* things worked:
  "How do I do this? How does this work?"
- The remainder wanted to explore future consequences. They were more interested in the *What if?*:
  "What would happen if I did this? What would happen if I didn't do this? What wouldn't happen if I did this?"

In the 1970s, Bernice McCarthy realised that most of the material the children were being given at school fitted into just one of those questions: the *What?* – facts, information, data. Think about your own schooling for a moment. Most formal teaching was presenting you information about things, about people, about the world. Formal education concentrates on the *What?* category. This works fine for the children who have that particular learning style. But it doesn't work so well for the children in the other three categories.

The first plan Bernice McCarthy had was to discover the learning style for each child when they entered school, and then have four streams, so that each child would be taught in their preferred style.

- The *why* children would be given lots of reasons and explanations.
- The *what* children would be given lots of data and information.
- The *how* children would have practical hands-on experience, doing things.
- And the *what if* children would have more of a self-discovery learning style, with group discussions.

It was originally thought that this would be the most effective way of teaching children. However, through further research it was realised that this way of teaching would actually reduce children's flexibility, and that it would be far better to structure the education system so that it answered all four questions for all the children. That way, every student would have their preferred learning style, which would work really well for them, and they would also be exposed to the other styles, so that they would be increasing their learning flexibility.

As adults we maintain our preferred learning style, so we will find one particular style is the most comfortable for our way of working.

The 4MAT system

4MAT	Learning style	Percentage
Why ?	Discussion	35%
What?	Teaching	22%
How?	Coaching	18%
What if?	Self-discovery	25%

The percentages of people in the general population in the US falling into each category are shown in the table above. They are roughly evenly divided.

However, in any selected group, such as managers, sales people, accountants, scientists, sports people, and so on, there will usually be a bias toward one particular category of learning style. Some cultures have different biases. For example, if you are training or presenting to a German audience, you will find that they will want to accumulate a huge mass of data, and they won't feel happy until they have it.

If you say these percentages out loud to your audience, then the ones who write them down are more likely to be in the *what* category. They want the details, the facts, figures, and information. So when you say: "This is what you need to know . . . " out come the pens, and they start writing everything down.

"Why?" people

The *Why?* group learn best by discussing the reasons why. They want to know why something is worth doing: "Why would we need to know this stuff? Why bother to use it?" They like to explore the reasons for taking action before actually doing so.

"What?" people

The *What?* group learn best when you give them the information either orally or on the printed page. In presentations and trainings the *what* people are happiest when there is so much information, and they are frantically making notes, but they can't write fast enough to keep up! Their criterion of a good training is: "Plenty of handouts!" and masses of facts, figures, and statistics. The value of the training lies in the thickness of the manual.

In any particular training or a presentation you will have people in all four categories. If you start a presentation by giving everyone a lot of *What?* you find that the *Why?* people won't actually assimilate the information, because they haven't a reason for doing so. If you don't give them a reason, they may quietly sit there for the whole presentation, or even the whole training, waiting for a good reason. They need to be motivated by a why before they will get into the *what*.

"How?" people

The *How?* people learn best by doing. They aren't too bothered about the theory, or the reasons: "Let me at it. I'll soon have this down." They want to be trying things out, getting the feel – the hands-on approach. For example, when these people first get their hands on a computer, they spend no time reading the manuals. They just start clicking on anything to see what happens. As a trainer, you have a coaching role. Get them to do something, give them feedback on what they did, and then coach them on what they could be doing better.

In our NLP trainings, the *how?* preference is satisfied by doing exercises. So when you are training, first give some reasons why they would want to do the exercise; then give them the necessary information about what to do. And then have them run the exercise, so that they can try it out for themselves.

"What if?" people

The *What if?* people learn best through self-discovery. When they go off to do a training exercise, and you then observe them doing it, it may bear no resemblance to what you asked them to do. They may have changed bits of the exercise around or they may be doing something completely different, because they go into the exercise thinking:

> "I wonder what would happen if we just leave that step out?"
> "It would be interesting to see what happens if we did this the other way."
> "What would happen if we put this extra step in, or if we combined this with that other exercise?"

In general these people will be considering the consequences of making changes to the structure of the exercise, the consequences of doing it in another context, and any possible repercussions on themselves through not sticking to the guidelines. It is almost as if they are testing the boundaries: finding out where they are, where they could go and what is possible. The *what if* way of thinking is exemplified in the following:

> "What are the opportunities around what I am learning here, that nobody has ever thought of before?"

And in a more global context:

> "Who can I sell it to? I'm not interested in doing it myself. All I am interested in are the opportunities, and who would want to buy it."

Related systems

The 4MAT system is nothing new. The original work from Bernice McCarthy was in the 1970s. It also relates to Jung's psychological types, and reappears in Kolb's learning styles, and in the work of Honey and Mumford. Briefly they connect up as follows:

4MAT	Kolb	Honey and Mumford	Jung
Why?	Abstract	Reflector	Introvert
What?	Concrete experience	Activist	Extrovert
How?	Active experimentation	Pragmatist	Feeler
What if?	Reflective observation	Theorist	Thinker

Because these fundamental distinctions run throughout the human experience, they will have often been reinvented in different guises. But bringing it down to the four simple, basic questions is immediately more user-friendly, becoming instantly available to you. So this is about applying an existing way of thinking to a new area.

All four categories
In any presentation or training you need to ensure that you give the information in a way that is suitable for all four learning styles. And you need to do this in a particular order.

1. Start with the *whys*, because until you give reasons, the *why* people won't listen to the rest of the information. In a training, they won't be motivated to do the exercises, and they certainly won't contemplate the *what ifs*. It is as though they are 'on hold' until they have good reasons for engaging. Therefore always give the *whys* first.
2. Then give some *what* information. Obviously people need details before doing an exercise, or thinking about how they might use something.
3. Third, do the *how*. In a training, this is an exercise; in a presentation it might be talking them through how they could implement this information back in their own environment or workplace.
4. Last, you need to look at the consequences: What would happen if you did this? What would happen if you didn't? What is likely to happen if you deviate from the plan? And so on.

In trainings you can take care of the *what if* section by what you do after an exercise. When the group is seated again, just ask:

"What did you learn, what did you discover, what questions do you have?"

This satisfies the *what if* people. When you ask this composite question, you will often notice that certain people in the group have something to say, because this is how the *what if* people are able to satisfy themselves.

The structure of this training
We actually do one other piece before these four. We set a frame, by telling the group what is coming, so that they have a label, a box to put the whole thing in. We call this the '*little what*'. So the whole structure is:

This is what's coming, the overall frame; this is why you would want to use it; this is what it is; this is how you use it; and these are the consequences if you do.

What this means in our way of teaching is that for every major section of a training, and for this book as well:

- The first thing to do is to provide a *little what*. For example, "Now we are going to explore the 4MAT System."
- And then: "This is why you would want to know this," and give some reasons for knowing about it.
- Then, the information – the knowledge, the data, the facts. "This is where it comes from. This is what it is, these are the essential distinctions. Here are some other things it is related to. These are the key points."
- Then, we set up an exercise, and we ask you to do it.

If you are a trainer, you will notice that in any group there are certain people who are really itching to do a practical exercise so they can become familiar with the information by using it. Whereas other people will be saying, "I don't really need to do the exercise. I know what this is now", because they have the information, and that is sufficient.

- And when we come back from an exercise, we ask if there are any comments, any questions, any observations.

In every training you are taking people through this cycle many times. Doing this means that you are also having them experience all four ways of learning – which everyone has anyway – so that every person in the group, no matter what their preferred learning style is, has been satisfied.

Sales presentations
Think about using this if you do sales presentations, or selling on a one-to-one basis.

- Start your sales presentation with: "This is what we can do for you." That is your *little what* that puts a frame round it.

- "This is *why* you would want to know what we can do for you."
- "This is *what* we can actually do for you. Here are the details."
- "This is *how* it will work for you. This is how you can utilise it in your business right now to get results."
- "And these are the consequences if you do, and the consequences if you don't."
- Then you close.

That is how you can use the 4MAT system as a model for selling.

Exercise 23: Preliminaries and Preparation for Your Final Presentation

In Chapter 18, the last chapter in this book, you will find Exercise 27, the final exercise. In it, you will be asked to give a ten-minute presentation that includes everything you have been learning in this book. For that presentation you will need about five minutes worth of content. In the exercises you have been doing so far, content has been irrelevant because you have been learning the process. Finally, you will be putting some content in. This may be a short piece of the kind of material you have been using in any previous presentations or trainings, or something you want to use in the future. It could be a segment of a larger presentation, or a short stand-alone piece of something you are familiar with.

- Choose a topic that you might wish to present in the future, and select a segment that will take you about five minutes to talk about.

If you will be doing business presentations then perhaps you want to choose a topic that you would normally be presenting in a business context. Or if you are in education or teaching, it could be a part of a class that you want to take. You must have some content in order to engage in the process, so choose a topic that is important to you.

When you do your final presentation what matters is *how* you put it across, and how you put *yourself* across. So we suggest that you pick something with which you are very familiar and totally comfortable, even something you know by heart, so that you can concentrate on the process of putting it across, rather than having to think about content.

The four questions

When you have something you want to talk about, you need to do some preparation ahead of time. Think about the answers to the following four questions about the content of your presentation. Essentially the four questions are: *Why?*, *What?*, *How?*, and *What if?*

Think about the four questions from the point of view of someone in your audience.

Why would I want to know about this?
Why would I want to hear about this particular topic you are talking about? What's in it for me? Why is it important for me to know about this? What benefit is there for me in getting the information you are going to tell me?

In a specific context, or a particular environment, you may know why someone would want to know this particular information. Otherwise you are going to have to mind-read or guess the answer.

What is this all about?
What is the information? What are the facts? What are the essential details that I need to be aware of? What do I need to know about this so that I can understand, and make sense of what you are talking about?

How will it work for me?
How can I use it? What is the process for my using this? How am I actually going to do it? How can I use this right now? How can I use this information you are giving me in a practical sense? How do I implement these ideas?

What if I do use it?

What would happen as a result of my doing what you are saying? What might be the repercussions for me if I use this information you are giving me? What are the consequences of using it, what are the consequences of not using it? What are the future possibilities of continuing to use it?

Now the reason *why* you would want to think of the answers to those questions is because within any audience people will be asking these questions. *What* you will find is that some people have a preference for one particular question. In the audience as a whole you will have those who are continually asking the question Why? Those people who want facts and information and are continually asking the question What? Others will be sitting there wondering, "How am I going to use this? How does this work for me?" And the remainder are considering: "What are the consequences … ? What would happen if I did use this stuff? What becomes possible from using the material that we haven't yet realised?"

By structuring your presentation to answer all four questions, you will be able to satisfy everyone in the group.

This is the difference between *why?* and *what if?*

- *Why* is the hook you use to get people to stay and listen to what you want to say *right now*. Give them a reason why your presentation is worth listening to. Relate this to why the person is at your presentation in the first place. If they are not motivated to stay, they will go somewhere else, even if it is inside their own head.

- *What if* is about the *future* consequences, other possibilities, that come from knowing what you have told them. Once they have the information, they can start to speculate, and wonder about the future possibilities, and explore the ramifications of taking action.

As an example: The reason you need to know this is because you are ensuring that you will have everyone in the room with you for the whole presentation. In the past you may have had the experience of doing an entire presentation, giving people lots of information, and then someone in the audience said, "Why are we doing this?" Now it would be useful for you to avoid situations like that, wouldn't it? That is the *why*.

People assimilate information in different ways. Basically there are four different learning styles, and people will be asking these four questions, whether they are consciously aware of it or not. Every person will have a particular preference for one of these questions. That is *what* this is all about.

Think about *how* you can use this structure in your presentations so that you answer those questions before they are asked. Consider how the people in your audience can use this information, and how it may be implemented in their particular context. What would be the best way of presenting the information so that when they have it, they will be able to use it for themselves?

Finally, the *what if*: You may be thinking, "What if I started structuring my presentations this way; what would be the consequences of doing this?" One would be that every person in the room has been given the information in their most preferred format, which will enable them to learn more easily, and to assimilate the information they want from what you are saying. It will also avoid any future situations where people might say, "Well, you have given me all this information. How am I going to use it?" or, "Why would I want all this information?" because you will have already given them the answers.

4MAT preparation
So think about your five minutes of content. Take what you want to talk about, and structure it in this way, ready for when you do your final presentation exercise.

For the final presentation you will need the following

- Your *stories*: five metaphors. Find five short stories, each about one minute in length. The five stories may be some of the incident – point – benefits you have already been using. This is perfectly OK, because they are anecdotes, stories, or metaphors. So you may have already come up with five and not realised it.

- Your *content*: the five minutes of material you have already started thinking about, which you will have structured in this format.
- And as a bonus, you will find that there is a particular Satir category that goes with each segment of this 4MAT structure, which you can add in.

Giving a presentation at short notice

If you ever are in a situation where someone says to you:

"I am really pleased you're here. We have all these important people here from head office, and they are very interested in that research you have been doing. Will you come and give us a ten minute presentation on what you have been doing?"

Instead of thinking, "Help! I haven't done any preparation. I don't know what I am going to say!" you just need to consider:

"How do I structure a presentation of this information using the 4MAT system so that it is effective and appropriate for everyone in the group?"

This is how you do it

- You stand up, go into the trainer state, and so on, and start by giving a brief overview of what is to come. You say: "This is what I have been researching. This is the information I am going to give you."
- Put in the *whys*: "Now here is the reason why you would want to know about this. Let me tell you why this research is so important."
- Go on to the *what*. You say: "So let me give you the information on this. These are the facts and figures on the findings that came out of our research work. Here are the essential points . . . "
- Tell them *how* they can implement this information: "By using this information, this is how, within the company, we could get these particular results."

● And finish by exploring the *what ifs*: "Let's think about some of the future consequences of applying this information. If we were to start using this knowledge in the company right now, this is likely to happen. Let's explore some possible benefits for our business, that we are not currently getting, but which we could be getting in the future. And let's also consider some of the consequences of what will happen if we don't use it right now."

You have now put together a presentation that will match the learning style of everyone in the group, and you have nicely structured all of your information. It does not matter whether you have five minutes, 20 minutes, an hour or 20 days. Instantly, you can go in and deliver something that will work.

Chapter Fifteen
States for the Audience

Eliciting States

As a presenter, you will always be eliciting states within an audience. At every moment they are going to be in some particular physiological and emotional state, and this will affect how they are paying attention to you, how they are learning, and so on. But are they in the states you want them to be? As the presenter or trainer you want your audience to be in the ideal state for receiving and processing the information you are offering them. It is your job to make sure that they are in the most appropriate state, your responsibility to know how to do this.

The people in the audience are not there as neutral information collectors. Once you have rapport with the audience, you can then lead them through a whole series of different states. Unless your style of presenting means that you want your audience in a state of total passivity and boredom the whole time, you will want to maintain their interest throughout your training or presentation by providing variety and richness in the states they are in: low, quiet, meditative, thoughtful states, or high, energetic, excited states; states of curiosity, great motivation, and so on. Working with states means you will be fully engaging your audience's interest as you take them on a rollercoaster ride through a range of emotional feelings.

Setting the frame

Imagine what it would be like if, at the beginning of a sales presentation, you could elicit a state of curiosity in your audience, so that they would be really curious about what you had to offer. Suppose you could elicit in them a state of decisiveness at the very moment you are closing the deal . . . By having them feeling decisive, they are more likely to be able to choose easily, one way or another, whether to buy what you are offering.

By eliciting a state of curiosity at the beginning of a training, you will have the people in the group curious about what you have to say. They will be enthusiastic to know about everything you are teaching them, and motivated to find out more about it. Consequently you will have their attention the whole time. That would be worth having, wouldn't it?

The ability to elicit states within an audience will take you from just being a good provider of information, to being an entertaining and captivating presenter. We strongly believe that if you are going to stand up in front of an audience, you had better be entertaining. Because if you aren't, why would people choose to be there? Why bother attending a live training when they could get the information from reading a book or listening to a tape? An audience wants to be entertained, and part of the entertainment comes from the states you are eliciting within them.

Using metaphors in training

Several years ago David was being trained to be a business coach. Thirteen trainees were sitting round a table with the trainer, who knew the power of telling stories and anecdotes, and was coaching people using metaphors. The trainer said "I want each of you to come up with a metaphor that you could use in a training. And we will go this way around the group". That definitely elicited a state within David: "Help! I'm no good at telling stories. I don't even know any stories". Fortunately David was in 13th position, so he thought, "OK, this gives me plenty of time to rack my brains for a story".

The first person told a great metaphor. Then the second person told an even better story. As this carried on round the table, every story and metaphor was surprising – it was so good – and David wondered how he could match this level of quality.

Now we don't know about you, but often when people are telling metaphors or stories, it's possible to drift off into your own little world; your attention goes inside, and you start dreaming. Various thoughts come drifting through your consciousness, your mind scrolls through past memories, and it is as though the training room and all the people telling their metaphors, disappear.

Here's an example from one of our trainings of Tad's use of state elicitation with a metaphor:

'The Sword in the Stone'
This particular radio play was about Merlin and Arthur. Tad has always been fascinated by Merlin and King Arthur, wizards, and all things magical. So he thought, "Ah. I'll listen to this for a while". We don't know if you have ever listened to plays on the radio, but what happens is that you enter into the world of the story, and even though there are no pictures as there are with television, you start making up your own pictures. So there he is in the world of King Arthur and Merlin, listening to the story, the play on the radio.

Arthur had been studying with Merlin for several years, learning how to do various magical things, and now the time had come for him to go out on his own and do his job, which essentially was to save the country. There was a task he had to do. In the middle of a very large rock, a sword was stuck. You may know the name of the sword. It was called *Excalibur*. And the sword was deep in the stone.

Merlin said to Arthur:

> "I have taught you many things. Even though you may be think-
> ing you can't do them all, it's now time for you to prove to
> yourself that you can. You have to take the sword from the stone,
> go out, and achieve many magical things."

But Arthur was not so sure. He was standing there looking at the sword in the stone, feeling rather hesitant, thinking about what he had to do. He knew the task he had to do was crucial, but he was hesitant about whether he could actually do it. Have you ever had that feeling of hesitation, knowing that what you have to do is so important that you are holding yourself back somehow, you are reluctant to start?

Now Merlin had learned quite a lot about the way people managed to achieve certain things, and as he watched Arthur, he was wondering, "What can I do to assist young Arthur in accomplishing what he wants to do?" He said to the hesitating Arthur:

"Well, Arthur, how do you want to be instead? I mean, what do you want to be like as far as this task I have given you is concerned?"

Arthur answered:

"I just want to take that sword from the stone. I want to hold it in my hands. Because then I will know absolutely that I can do anything I want to do. Anything."

Have you ever had, even for a moment, that feeling: "I can do anything I want; I know everything I need to know; and I can just go ahead and do it?" Or can you imagine feeling that you knew you could do anything you wanted? That is what Arthur wanted to feel like.

Arthur was hesitating again, so Merlin said:

"When you hesitate, what is it that stops your hesitating? Because something must stop your hesitating, otherwise you wouldn't be here. So when you hesitated before, what was it that got you out of the hesitation?"

Arthur pondered on this:

"Well, the thing is I just get so frustrated with myself. Because I know I can do it. I have seen other people do it. So I start trying to do it, and I put all my energy into trying to make it happen. But I just get so frustrated with myself, because what I am doing isn't working."

Have you ever been that frustrated with yourself about something? I mean really frustrated? Can you imagine the sort of frustration that Arthur was feeling at that moment? He was so frustrated it was as if he were going to explode!

Merlin, being in the trainer state, of course, feeling nice and calm and relaxed, simply acknowledged this feedback from Arthur, and said:

"Well, then what happens Arthur? You're frustrated. But what happens next? Obviously you don't stay frustrated all the time. You must come out of it, into another feeling or another state."

Arthur thought about this:

"Well, it's as though after a while it reaches such a point that there is nothing I can do. I am so overloaded with frustration that I can't hold on any more, and I have to let go of all that. And when I do, things begin to flow again. I get some ideas and things begin to take off again. It dawns upon me that I am starting to get it."

Have you ever had an experience like that, where you have been holding on, keeping everything in, and it has built up so much that you are totally blocked, not going anywhere? And suddenly it is as though you have gone over the threshold, and you think, "I give up!" and you let everything go. And then you have a sense of things naturally flowing again, because you are no longer in the way. D'you know that kind of feeling? It's a feeling of knowing things are moving, you're not fully there yet, but you're on the way.

Merlin said to Arthur:

"When you know what result you want, what do you do between having the first dawning of the idea, and actually doing the thing you want to do?"

A wry smile came onto Arthur's face:

"Well, once I have let go of trying to do things, it just happens. I feel part of the process, at one with things, rather than trying to force anything against its will. And then things just naturally happen."

Arthur was just going over in his mind what he actually did, because he had not thought of it in this way before. He knew he was very hesitant at first, because he knew that what he had to do was really important. So then he tried doing lots of things, but the more he tried, the less he actually achieved, and he got frustrated. Really frustrating himself, almost about to burst! But then he took

195

a deep breath, and let everything go. His entire physiology changed: he released the tension, got out of his own way, and then suddenly everything changed, and he was thinking, "Now it's happening. I am simply guiding the energy to where it wants to go".

And as soon as he got this piece about going with the flow of things, he knew what to do. As he stayed in this easy, relaxed state, he reached out for the sword, took it in both hands – and he slid it out of the stone as though he were releasing it from a scabbard. And now he stood there with the sword in his hands.

And if anybody were to look at Arthur at that particular moment, they would know that here was a person who knew he could do absolutely anything.

*   *   *   *   *   *   *

As he tells this story, Tad is moving around the stage and linking certain states with different locations. Essentially he is establishing associations between four spots along the front of the stage, with each of Arthur's four states:

● Hesitation
● Frustration
● Letting go
● Realisation.

Now, the conclusion:

'The Sword no longer in the Stone'
So, Arthur stood there, holding Excalibur in his hands, realising that he really could do anything he wanted to do. Then he had another realisation. Previously, he'd thought that the only way he could go out and do anything was if he had Excalibur in his hands. But as soon as he held it in his hands, he realised it had nothing to do with Excalibur at all. Because all of the power that he thought was in Excalibur was actually inside himself. And for all that Excalibur was, it was just a tool. And really the place where all the power came from was inside him. Inside Arthur. So

he realised that he could always do whatever he wanted to do. He could always achieve whatever he wanted to achieve, no matter whether he had the tools, or the techniques; it was all in here inside him anyway.

Eliciting States in an Audience

Let's look at four ways of eliciting states within one person, or in an audience. As always, for these to work, you must establish rapport before doing anything else.

1. ***Go into the desired state yourself***

    When you are in rapport with someone, they will start matching your state. If, for example, you go into a state of motivation, then they are naturally going to follow you, and become motivated themselves. This is what rapport is really about. Once you have made the connection with them, by matching them, they will maintain the connection and match you – for as long as they are comfortable.

    You have to be able to demonstrate the state you want, to 'walk your talk'. You can't fake it, because if you are not in the state yourself, they won't be in it either. For example, suppose you want to motivate a group. You are in rapport with them, you're sitting down, and you casually say to them:

    "I don't know. Do you want to do this, or not? What d'you think? Or shall we do it tomorrow? I suppose we could do that. I mean, can you remember a time when you thought you were kind of motivated? Wouldn't it be great to get motivated right now? Yeah. Shall we do it . . . ?"

    This laid-back style is not going to work. You have to go into a motivated state yourself if you want to get them motivated. It only happens when you yourself are fired up. And you then say enthusiastically:

"Remember a time when you were totally motivated, like you were really going for it. A time when you just couldn't help yourself, you just had to do it."

When you get into the state, they will follow you into the state themselves. You may have seen this with motivational speakers. Now you know why they are doing that.

2. *Ask the audience to remember a time in the past when they were in the desired state.*
Ask people to remember an occasion in the past when they were in that desired state. Because as soon as they do remember such a time they will get the feelings that go along with the memory of what happened. Just activating the memory will put them back in that particular state again. Do this now:

● Think of a time in the past when you felt really excited. And when you have an example of that, just run that memory in your mind, see it again in your mind's eye, and be aware of the feelings . . . When you do this, you will get excited again to some extent.

3. *Ask them to imagine a time in the future when they will be in the desired state.*
You can also have people imagine a time in the future when they would be in the desired state. You may have to help by painting for them a mental picture of what it would be like. However, remembering a past experience is always pre-ferred, because it will have more 'reality' and therefore more impact.

There may be times when you need to go into the future, though. We were once talking about motivation with a group of people in a particular company, and said to them:

"Remember a time in the past when you were really moti-vated, really fired up, totally going for it."
"No. No we can't."
"Come on, there must have been some time in the past when you were totally motivated."

"Obviously you don't work here."

We realised, "Whoops! We're not going to get paid for this unless we resolve this one." So instead we had them imagine a time in the future when they would be motivated:

"Well, can you imagine being motivated? Think of a time in the future when you are really going for it."
"Oh, yeah. We can definitely do that."

Then we had something to work with, because they could imagine a time in the future having the desired state. But given the choice, a past memory is always preferable to a future one, because a remembered experience produces a stronger state.

4. *Tell them a story or metaphor*
All stories and metaphors evoke states, which is why people like hearing stories, why they go to the cinema to see action movies, horror movies, comedies, or romances. It is why when you were a kid you liked reading storybooks, or having stories read to you, because a story evokes thoughts in your mind, and these thoughts elicit states in your body. Every story you tell to your audience will elicit a particular state within each person in the audience.

Universal Experiences

So how do you know that the state you elicit in the audience will be the one that you want? People's responses vary widely, because no two people have had exactly the same experience. So what do you do?

You have the highest probability of eliciting the state you want within an audience, or within one person, by using the phrase, "Remember a time when . . . " and telling them about some *universal experience*. A 'universal' experience is one that you can reasonably guarantee at least 80% of the people in the room will have experienced at some time. One example of a universal experience is the story about sneaking in and peeking at your

Christmas presents when you were a kid. Most kids have done that. And everybody has been a kid – that's guaranteed. So the chances are they will have had the experience of getting curious about their presents, finding them, and investigating them. Just by mentioning it they will remember their own experience, and their curiosity will come back.

Other examples of universal experiences are:

- being in a group of people;
- being alone;
- being lonely;
- going on a journey;
- arriving in a new place;
- being ill and being looked after;
- being surprised;
- having to wait for something;
- losing something important;
- finding something valuable;
- having a argument or a fight;
- regretting doing something;
- being confused;
- learning something significant;
- having an amazing coincidence; and so on.

Everyone has had these experiences at some time in their lives, and probably many times. And there are many universal cultural experiences we frequently encounter, such as eating in restaurants, or driving cars in towns, and stopping at traffic lights. And how about this one:

You are standing in line at the bank during your lunch break, and you have only five minutes before you have to be back for an important meeting. You wanted to join the fastest moving line, so you picked one with only two people in front of you. You look at your watch, and think, "I've another three minutes. I should still be able to do it". Then the person in front of you gets their turn at the teller, and you suddenly realise they are a shop owner. And they have a huge bundle of cheques, and a large bag of cash that has to be counted . . .

That is a fairly common experience. Similarly:

You are waiting in the checkout line in the supermarket, and the person in front of you has bought something without a price label, and a store assistant has to walk to the appropriate aisle at the other end of the shop … And you are screaming inside: "Come on, come on! I can't wait all day!"

These are the kinds of state that will drive people to do something.

Exercise 24: Universal Experiences

It is worth having a stock of stories or metaphors about these universal experiences – appropriate to the kind of training or presenting you are doing – so that you can create various states in your audience by telling them. Therefore it is good idea to collect stories that you can tell as and when the need arises. You already know some of the ones we use, and you can adapt them as you wish. In the next exercise you will be gathering some more universal experiences to expand your repertoire.

This is what you do:

- Get with your practice group and brainstorm universal experiences. You are going for quantity. Brainstorming means that you come up with as many examples as possible within the time, but there is no evaluation or discussion about them. That comes later.
- Focus on: what are some experiences which you can guarantee that at least 80-90% of people, in a particular audience, will have had at some time. For example, if you usually present to a business audience, what are some universal business experiences? Or for educators, what are some universal experiences that are part of teaching and education?
- You need to be able to be certain that at least 80% of the people in the group will have a similar response to these universal experiences. There may well be experiences which are positive for you, but the rest of the people in the group

will be thinking, "Oh, no! That's the worst thing I could ever imagine".

● Then, for each item on your list of universal experiences, predict the state it will elicit within your audience. If you were to tell your audience about that particular experience, what state would it elicit?

● As you go through this process, you may find that you want to make some changes, or do some editing to your list. That is OK.

Take about 20 minutes to do this exercise with your group now. Of course, you can always add more experiences to your list whenever you think of them.

Debrief

We live in a society that is hooked on stories. And this is more than just bedtime stories for children, the novels we read, or the soaps we watch on television. We are all employing metaphors and stories all the time. When we get together with our friends we tell stories: accounts of recent holidays, problems with the car, or what happened at the game. Go to the cinema, turn on the television: it is all stories. Newspapers and news bulletins actually deal in news *stories*. Our media and entertainment industries are huge, and constantly feed our need for more and more stories. We would even go so far as to say that stories are essential in our lives. They are certainly a very powerful way of learning. And even though we may think of scientific knowledge in terms of facts, when we look more closely it is all framed in terms of stories: *The Origin of Species, The Double Helix, The Blind Watchmaker, A Brief History of Time,* and so on: stories of evolution, genetic engineering, physics and space exploration, medical research, the destruction of the ozone layer, and so on. We learn about and understand these things through stories and metaphors at various levels of sophistication.

Therefore telling relevant stories is an essential part of your presentations and trainings. And you have the whole range of human experience to draw on. If something is meaningful and memorable, then it probably contains some learning points, which you can bring out, depending upon the spin you give it. You need to know what you want to achieve by telling the story. Then you can change the emphasis you put on it, or the frame you put around it, so that it will work for the audience in front of you. Telling metaphors and stories will elicit certain states in the audience. You may use the same story to elicit a whole series of states, just from the way you tell it. You have already experienced this by telling your stories in the different sensory systems. You may have realised that this is much easier than you first thought.

By telling a sequence of stories, then, depending how you sequence them, you can lead people through a series of different states during your presentation or training. This is what good stand-up comedians do in their acts.

Predicting the Response

When you want to use these universal stories in a presentation, consider carefully:

● Can I accurately predict that the majority of the people in the group are going to have a similar response?

It is not always easy to predict the state elicited by certain universal experiences. For example, the birth of the child has a range of associated emotions: some possibly quite traumatic, while others delightful and joyous. So you need to set the scene by referring to a specific aspect of the experience that is relevant. And you will of course be accessing that state yourself, so that the audience will pick it up.

Birthday parties are usually times for great fun and excitement, and also of curiosity beforehand. There may even be frustration from waiting and wondering what is going to happen at the party: Will you get presents you will like? Who is going to be there? What might they do to surprise you? So you need to be quite specific on which aspect of the event will elicit the state you want.

If you tell a story that you think is really good, but then notice that some of the audience are frowning, shaking their heads, somehow expressing, "No way!" or whatever, then this is feedback for you. You are getting some responses, but are they the responses you want? You may need to do something else to shift their state. If you are not getting what you intended, change the story in some way so that it produces a different response. Or tell a different story. And remember, if something flops, you now know what to do. Step out of that 'story telling space' on the stage and dissociate yourself from what has just happened. You could say something like, "Do you believe that story?" and then move on to something you know will change the group's state to one you want.

Don't think that all the states you elicit have to be 'nice' ones. For example, frustration is a useful state to elicit in an audience every now and again. If you want the audience to be fired up, ready to go and do an exercise, then a frustration story will be very motivating.

Chapter Sixteen
Embedded Metaphors

Embedded metaphors tell the audience: You don't have it all yet.

To maintain the audience's interest and attention so they remain open to learning new things, you must let them know that they don't have all the information yet: there is more to come, things are still open. They have some pieces, but they don't know everything there is to know on that particular topic – yet. And you will continue to have their attention until they think they have the final piece.

We call this process of setting things up such that the audience knows, either consciously or unconsciously, that they don't have it all yet, *opening loops*. Thinking you know everything there is to know about something is really not a useful place to be because it prevents you from learning more. Opening loops prevents premature closure.

One way that we use to keep the audience open and anticipating more, so that they are taking in everything you have to say, and wanting to know more, is by telling stories – but in a special way, which we call embedded metaphors or *nested loops*. We recommend that you incorporate these into your own trainings and presentations.

Figure 16.1

Nested loops

You start telling a story, a metaphor, or an anecdote, but you don't complete it before starting another story. And then you tell only part of a second story before moving onto a third, and so on. This is known as opening nested loops. You only close the loops much later, by finishing each of the stories in reverse order (*Figure 16.1*).

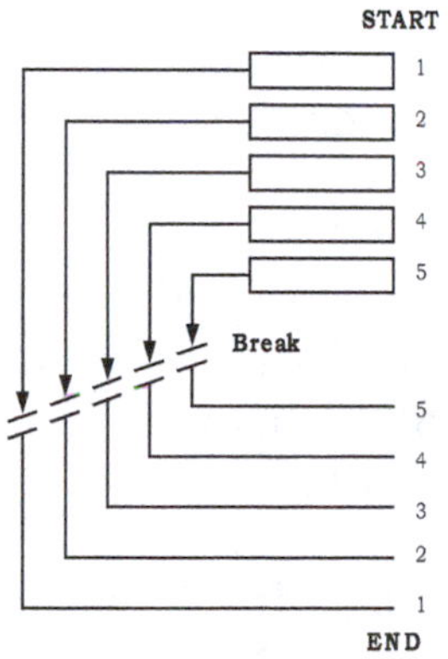

This is what you do:

- Start telling one of your stories, and about 75–95% of the way through you break off, so there is no resolution, punch-line, or conclusion.
- You immediately lead into another story. And again you tell only part of it before breaking off to start a third story. And you don't finish that story either. You leave all three stories incomplete.

You could go on and do stories four and five, but three is enough to start with. Three is the minimum number. The maximum is up to you – how much time you have, how well you can track the stories over time. In our longer trainings, we will have far more than three stories.

The purpose in breaking off these stories before they are completed is that people then know they haven't got the end of the story, they don't have a sense of completion, or even know the point of the story. They know there is more to come. This will create states of anticipation, attention, curiosity and wanting to know more – which are useful states to elicit for your presentations or trainings.

Nesting stories like this is not something peculiar to our trainings and presentations. We all do this occasionally. When you are telling your friends about the events in your life: what happened at work, when you were away on holiday, or whatever, quite often you tell part of a story and get distracted, or something will remind you of another incident, and you start following that track. And then you reach some point in that story, and get diverted again, and your story branches. As you start following this new line of thought, your friends may say: "Hang on a minute, what happened to . . . ?" Have you ever had that happen?

The course of many a conversation twists and branches, as each participant steers the topic of conversation where they want it to go. When one person comes to an event that triggers memories off in someone else, they come in with their story, which then reminds you of something, and you take over and tell them about your incident, which then reminds them of . . . People are naturally familiar with nested loops in their everyday conversations and creating that kind of "serial incompleteness".

Here's an example of how to do this:

From a presentation at the annual convention of the American Board of Hypnotherapy by Tad James
February 13, 1994: Irvine, California.

Introduction

When your clients come to see you, they come with a presenting problem, they kind of have an idea of what the problem is, but they're not really sure they have an unconscious mind. Sometimes, our main job is to get them in touch with THEIR UNCONSCIOUS. A lot of times it's simply for them to discover that very deep part of themselves, an unconscious mind. Not the conscious mind. Because if they could have done what they were doing with their conscious mind already, they would have . . . you see. See, they already would have taken the time if they could, already would have discovered what they needed to discover, but they weren't able to do that, right away. Yet when they come to us, one of the things that we'll need to do then, is assist them in getting in touch with that unconscious part of them, their UNCONSCIOUS MIND.

So one of the major pieces of Ericksonian hypnosis is that you do have an UNCONSCIOUS MIND. Is anyone here aware of that *(laughter)* Good . . . Good . . . OK. And one of the key principles of Ericksonian hypnosis is, and of course in the old days, in the authoritarian approach to hypnosis, of course the hypnotist used to say . . . "Uncross your legs, put your hands on your knees, take a deep breath *(breathe in)* and go deeply asleep." Of course, we don't have to say that anymore. Knowing ERICKSONIAN HYPNOSIS, what we've discovered is, knowing, ambiguity in any sense will assist us in communicating with the unconscious mind. Ambiguity in any sense will assist us in communicating more directly with the unconscious mind.

Open Loop #1

Now it took Erickson a long time to develop this. Think about this for just a minute. He was in practice doing hypnosis every single day, from about 1920 until his death in 1980. And during that period of time of 60 years, he would see upwards of 14 patients a day, sometimes seven days a week. Now, the way I see it, if you did that, you'd get pretty good at hypnosis too. You'd figure out what to do after a while, and what Erickson said was, he said, "It took me a long time to learn this". He said, "But once I learned it, my hypnosis became a lot better", and "I was much more easily able to facilitate trance in my clients". And I realised that most of what needs to happen in hypnosis is utilisation. We need to discover and utilise already occurring phenomena that the client brings to the hypnotic session. And so he said, "Whereas during the early days, I was very fond of telling the client what to do, and I would really say, 'Go into a trance'", he said, "I don't say that anymore". He said, in fact, "One of the things I did in the process of learning how to communicate with the UNCONSCIOUS MIND was", he said, "that I, in the early days, is, that I actually sat down at a typewriter and typed out 30 type-written pages of notes. Imagine that. Single-spaced, narrow margins, wide type on the page, type-written pages, of all the ways I could figure out how to GO INTO A TRANCE, easily. And", he said, "with experience I was able to reduce that as I continued my practice to 25 pages, and then 20, and then 15, and then ten, and then nine, eight, pages, and then seven, then six, then five, and then, um, um, *(laughter)* three, and then two, and then one, and then", he said, "I could reduce it to one paragraph, and then one sentence, and then", he said, "I realised I didn't need to use words at all. And what I could do is really by utilising the naturally occurring states in a client, I could begin to assist the client to GO DEEPLY INTO A TRANCE".

Open Sub-Loop #1a

Now this was an interesting learning for him. He started out more authoritarian than most. In fact some people who analyse Erickson say he had pretty high control needs. As time went on however, he realised that he could simply utilise naturally occurring things that were going to happen. For example: In just a moment you'll blink *(laughter)*, and if you blink, THAT'S RIGHT, just after I say, "go ahead and blink" THAT'S RIGHT, then YOUR UNCONSCIOUS.

> ### Open Sub-Loop #1b

By the way, some people ask me, "Tad, why do you use the word unconscious instead of subconscious, or, as some people in the northwest say, other-than-conscious?" Pardon me, The reason why I say, YOUR UNCONSCIOUS mind, is first of all, that's what Erickson said, and I know of no better way to look at a client and say, "You know, YOUR UNCONSCIOUS mind" *(laughter)*.

> ### Open Sub-Loop #1c

So, one of the things that's really important, and, by the way, those of you taking notes, have you ever noticed how your pen sometimes . . . In fact, I remember one time when I was in college and I'd sort of been, you know how it is in college . . . you play . . . and one of those days in class, and I was writing along taking notes, and I had this profound dissociation where my hand looked like someone else's hand, you know, and, wow, that's really bizarre . . . 'cause that doesn't even look like my hand. I'm sure it wasn't TRANCE. But it probably was because I was TIRED AND SLEEPY.

> ### Close Sub-Loop #1c

And so I was writing along, you know, and my pen at one point began writing without me. Did you ever do that, and then you know you try to stay awake, and your eyelids get . . . Have you ever been tired like that, and you say, "I'm really going to stay awake, then YOUR EYELIDS GET REALLY, REALLY HEAVY, And you're just sitting there writing, and all of a sudden the sleep spindles come and ... you go ... WAHHNA ... "

Close Sub-Loop #1b

... and you don't want the professor to think you're sleeping ... in his class. So, you try, and you REALLY try, in vain to stay awake. And you're writing and all of a sudden you're ... did you ever notice how sometimes you're ... did you ever fall asleep when you're writing, and the characters just sort of dribble off into nothing, and then kinda down the page? Anyway, here I am in class, trying to stay awake, and I'm writing along like that, that's right, and ... that's right ...

Close Sub-Loop #1a

You know, YOUR UNCONSCIOUS ... mind *(laughter)*.

And so what's really important as we begin to discuss Ericksonian hypnosis is that ability to look at people. I said this in the class I taught a couple of days ago, I said, "One of the things I'm going to suggest as we do this kind of therapeutic intervention for a client, is that you actually look at the person across from you, and because in order to utilise ... for example, and you'd say to a client, 'And you may not have noticed this as you sat here, but your breathing has slowed down, your respiration has become more shallow, for some of you, you've begun to attain that sort of waxy flexibility that's known as the beginning stages of arm catalepsy ... ' not yet, but certainly notice that a lot of times you can begin to see certain changes occur in not only yourself but also the client, as you do". And so the notion of utilisation depends upon paying attention to certain things.

And if I could give you a gift, it would be a gift of curiosity. Of course, a gift of curiosity is always my favourite thing for hypnotherapists."

Now, Freud didn't care about this. In fact Freud had learned hypnosis but he had false teeth that didn't fit very well ... bless his heart ... so he wasn't able to do hypnosis as well as some of the other folks in town. So he created the talking therapy, where he put the client behind him, where the client could not see him, and I suspect, where he also would not have to look at the client. Too much. But in hypnosis, when you're in hypnosis, then I'm going to suggest that you look at your client. And the things you can see.

> Open Loop #2

And what will facilitate this is a profound curiosity. I don't know if you remember when you were a kid, but when I was a kid, my dad used to hide the Christmas presents in the closet in his bedroom. And I always wanted to know what they were. Didn't you? So, I'd wait ... I grew up in Syracuse where there's lots of snow, fortunately, so they would go outside and shovel the driveway, and I'd run over to the bedroom, over to my Dad's closet, and I'd pull up a chair, then I'd look and see how they were doing ... Then I'd run back and reach way up and grab the big present. And what's the first thing you'd do? Shake it. 'Cause you want to know what's inside. Then you'd look at the outer wrapper. And you could tell a lot of things from outer wrappers, couldn't you? You could. Like, was the box heavy, was the paper thin? Which store did it come from? After a while you'd begin to notice that certain wrappers had certain different characteristics, that you could see things. And, if you really got daring, and if you felt you had a lot of time, from time to time, you'd occasionally peel the paper back carefully, hoping not to rip the wrapping. You did, I know you did ... Hoping not to rip the wrapping paper and then you'd look inside. If I could give you a gift, it would be that kind of curiosity, that kind of curiosity about what in the world is going on over there, as you look at the client.

So, pay attention to your client, as you see what's going on across from you. And if the client begins to exhibit behaviour which looks like ... THAT'S RIGHT, trance, then the first thing you can say is THAT'S RIGHT ... Or anything like that that acknowledges the behaviour. Now from the point of view of behavioural conditioning, every time we say THAT'S RIGHT, when the client does something that we're asking the client to do, such as ... GO VERY DEEPLY INSIDE, all the while HEARING THE SOUND OF MY VOICE, then if we say, THAT'S RIGHT, when they do, what they'll experience is a very profound alteration in consciousness. A very profound shift. So utilisation of naturally occurring states is very important.

Now one of the things that's useful when doing this is also utilisation of everything that's going on around you. It's really important to do that. As you're sitting here, of course from time to time as you listen carefully to what I'm saying, you may hear the sounds of other voices, perhaps the voice behind you, and some from outside, you may hear the rattling of paper, as your neighbour changes her page, or you may just hear the rustling or maybe your own breathing. As you listen carefully to what I am saying. And all of that. Now what I'm doing is I'm utilising things you've already heard, then I'm linking that to a suggestion. AND ALL OF THAT CAN MAKE YOU FEEL VERY ... RELAXED NOW ... AND COMFORTABLE. AND VERY VERY COMFORTABLE ... THAT'S RIGHT ... JUST GO DEEPLY ... THAT'S RIGHT ... VERY GOOD ... AND REALLY BE COMFORTABLE ... GOOD ... So utilizing what's happening in your client is a major part of Ericksonian hypnosis. Remembering that it's not just your conscious mind, that you want to be talking to, it's YOUR UNCONSCIOUS. And the other reason why I use the term UNCONSCIOUS MIND is because YOUR UNCONSCIOUS DOESN'T MIND. So, utilisation, extremely important. In fact.

Erickson tells this wonderful story, In fact, I think it's written up in a book, *My Voice will Go With You,* by Jeffery Rosen, which I think is one of the courses. If you haven't read it, I think you really ought to.

Open Loop #3

And, Erickson told a story about one of his students who was very interested in learning about hypnosis . . . And really wanted to learn how to, and so what he would do, Erickson told his student . . . we'll call him John as an example . . . what Erickson would do is he would really tell John to pay very close attention, very close attention to the people around him. John was in college and so one day the professor came to John and said, "John, how will you do on the test?" And John said, "I shall do very well professor, because you only have 10 questions, and they are . . . " John proceeded to name the 10 questions. Now the professor was shocked, because he thought that John was an honourable man, and he said to John, "John, you've obviously gone into my desk, because not only do you know the 10 questions, but you knew them in order. We are going to the dean. So he took John to the dean and the dean said: "John, have you been cheating?" And John said, "No I haven't and I can prove it. Please send someone to my room to get my notebook". So, they sent someone to John's room to get his notebook, and brought it back and opened it up. John had taken very, very good notes. And next to some things he'd put one *, and next to some things he'd put 2*, and next to some things he'd put 3*, and next to some . . . of the things John had put 4*, and next to some things he'd put 5, and next to some 6, but only next to some things did John put 7*, and they weren't numbered. 1.2.3.4.5. No, No. The first one was 6, the second was 3, and the third one was 4, and the 4th one was 2, and so on. And John said, "You know, you can tell a lot by paying attention to what a professor is saying, because they all have their own ideas about what they like and what they don't like", and he said, "So all I did was pay attention, and listen carefully to his tone of voice, and look at him ..." You know, Erickson thought that John was one of his best students. Now in fact, he was always telling students to pay attention to things they normally did not pay attention to. Always telling students to pay attention to things they didn't pay attention to.

For example, as you think about it, of course there's lots of things going on simultaneously in your awareness. That's right. Simultaneously, you might be hearing the sound of my voice, and seeing the things in the room, but all the while certain sensations going on inside, and not just of increasing comfort and relaxation, but other things inside. That's right ... Very good ... Where you know that you're awareness is turning within, but all the while paying close attention to my voice, and that's not just metaphorical by the way. That's useful to say from time to time when you talk to your client. And so Erickson would ask people to pay attention to things that they hadn't ... Good job ... otherwise they paid attention to whether they were awake, or not. And, paying close attention to those things that one doesn't always pay attention to inside, like sensations for example.

In fact, there's a funny story.

Open Loop #4

One time a husband and wife came to Erickson. The husband had a wooden leg, but he had phantom leg pain. You know, pain in the leg where there was no leg. Imagine that. Leg pain in the leg where there was no leg. Did you ever think of that? The guy was having leg pains in the leg where there was no leg. Like, for example, if you didn't have a foot, and then you'd feel something in the foot. He was paying attention to things like that. And there was no foot there. And his wife was complaining of tinnitus. That's ringing in the ears, you know. And one of the things he said to each of them, he said, "Pay attention to what's going on". He said, "But if you can have phantom leg pain in the leg where there is no leg, then you can have good feelings there too, simply by tuning your awareness slightly, you can begin to feel things that aren't immediately obvious. That's right. Very good. And of course to his wife, who had the ringing in the ears, he knew she was a piano player, so he asked her to play a different tune. Inside.

Open Loop #5

Now, one of my of course favourite stories, and you'll probably hear me do this from time to time, is that one day Erickson was walking down the street in the town where he lived, and he heard from over there somewhere, a noise. And he said, I think there's something to learn here. So he looked in the direction of the noise, and he saw a building and a large sign on top the building that said, 'So-and-So Boiler Factory'. So he went across the street, and looked at the sign, and as he went inside, he could feel the tug of the door in his hand as he stepped over the threshold, and then he went inside. And when he got inside, he said, the noise was so tremendous. And he could see the workers, and they were all purposefully going back and forth inside this boiler factory, but he couldn't hear them. I don't know if you know this but in those days, they used to make big boilers. Like imagine a boiler the size of this room. Can you? A boiler the size of this room, with sheets of steel, maybe an inch or two thick, and rivets along the top, and maybe there would be one rivet every two feet, or two rivets every 18 inches, or maybe three rivets every foot, along the top, and then riveting the ends, sealing in the ends, so that, if you could imagine us being in a boiler like that, those were the kind of boilers they were making in this boiler factory. And so, Erickson when he got inside, he said, "There's got to be something to learn here, because those people are communicating inside, and I can't hear them, but they could hear each other, but he couldn't hear them inside". That's right. And so, he said, "I've got to learn something about this". So he stopped one of the workers and he said, "Can you get me the boss. Ask the boss to come outside so I can speak to the boss". The first worker he asked didn't know what to do, so he asked another worker, "Can you get me the boss? Can you ask the boss to come outside so we can have a discussion?" The boss came outside and Erickson said, "I'd like to sleep here for the evening . . . I'm a student and I'm learning how to communicate inside the boiler factory". And then Erickson said. "So, I'd like to sleep here for the evening". Now in those days, I guess it was all right, 'cause the boss said OK. So Erickson went home and got his pillow and his blanket, and he went back into the boiler factory, and he said he went across the steps and pulled the door open and once again, all of a sudden, there was all this noise inside. Each time he went inside, he could hear all this noise ... the workers going back and forth, the sheets of steel moving on the conveyors, and the rivets riveting. He said, "For the life of me, I almost couldn't hear myself think". He said, "But I managed to find a place out of the way. So I laid out my pillow and my blanket, and, since it was a little cool, I got under the blanket ... snuggled up ... but even so the noise inside was in my head ... loud as ever. But round about midnight, I managed to take all the noise and put it outside my head, and then I fell asleep. Very good".

Erickson was always putting himself in situations like that. Situations where he could learn. That's Right. Things. About what happens inside you. Not your conscious mind. Your unconscious ... and really unconscious ... and you don't mind, do you?

Central Content

Let me tell you if I may, such an honoured group as yourselves, knowing about your unconscious mind. I'd like to say that we have a wonderful, wonderful device at our beck and call, and that wonderful device is your unconscious mind. And your unconscious ... mind is a wonderful, wonderful being. And see, your unconscious mind laughs when you laugh.

Your unconscious mind weeps when you weep. Your unconscious mind is in charge of your emotions. And it makes your body work. What a job. Would you make your heart beat every day, 60 times a minute. Would that be all you would do? But your unconscious mind does much more than that. It makes you breathe, your eyes blink, That's right. Very good, and you don't even have to think about it. Your digestion works, and everything works. And you know, your unconscious mind does all that for you, and yet have you thanked it recently? Have you said, "Hey, UNCONSCIOUS MIND, thank you for all you do for me"?

When Milton Erickson awoke the next morning inside the boiler factory the first thing he heard is the workers saying, "What does that kid think he can learn here, when it has taken us so long to learn how to communicate inside?" But he knew that he'd learned something very valuable. He knew he'd learned something that could carry him through his entire life. He knew because if you can communicate with your unconscious ... your unconscious mind, you can ask it to do anything. Clear up your health, have you be happy, be healthy. Just communicating with your UNCONSCIOUS MIND, at least that's what Erickson thought. I don't know ... perhaps: what do you think?

Close Loop #5

But the woman who had ringing in her ear, she said, "I've learned how to play a different tune". The man with phantom leg pain discovered that really if he had, really changed his feelings so he could feel something else now . . . he'd learned how to tune his awareness.

Close Loop #4

And so, the professor said, "John, since you knew all 10 questions and the order they were in, I believe you knew the answers", and the dean said, "I'm going to recommend that John gets an A in this course." In fact, Erickson said, John got all As because he knew how to pay attention to what was going on outside. He really knew how to look at people, and he knew that that was a learning he would remember the rest of his life. And remember it he did.

Close Loop #3

I never got caught looking at Christmas presents. I never did, I really never did. But they always knew. And now that you're a parent don't you know? There's that little telltale sign, of the slightly ripped paper and you think, "I guess I'd better change my hiding place next year." – But all the while that curiosity: Hey, what's going on in here? What's happening inside?

If I could give you a gift today, it would be that wonderful gift of curiosity. That wondering of, as you look over at your client . . . what in the world is going on in there? So as you pay attention to your clients, and really pay attention, and really begin to pay attention to your clients.

Close Loop #2

And as you go through your degree program and begin to develop those 30 pages that Erickson developed. But don't start with 30, start with one . . . and then two . . . three . . .

> and then, um ... five ... I must have been attending Dr Krasner's introductory weekends. There's a number missing here, one, two, three ... five. OK.
>
> | Close Loop #1 |
>
> And really pay attention to detail of inducing trance, and I can assure you a most rewarding experience.
>
> | Close |

Leaving metaphors unfinished

In all our training programmes, we open loops at the beginning of day one, and leave it open throughout the training. We close them at only the very end of the last day. This is true for our three-day, 20-day and modular trainings over three months, by which time people have probably not remembered what we have opened. But as soon as we start closing a story, instantly it is as though they are right back where we left them, days or months earlier, as if no time had passed. The nice thing about closing the stories at the end of the training is that it seals in everything you have covered in your time together. It packages the experience, and installs the information nicely within each person.

At the end of the training or presentation, what will happen is that each loop will be closed. Or rather, most of them will be closed.

Exercise 25: Five Stories or Metaphors

You will need to have this ready for the presentation exercises that follow.

- Come up with five short stories or metaphors that you could use in a presentation. These may be anecdotes or accounts of events that have happened to you or to someone else. They can be made-up or real stories based on your life experience. They could be personal, or about work or business.
- Keep your five stories short. They should take no longer than one minute to tell. You may need to edit your stories to keep them simple, to bring out the essential points.

All successful presenters and trainers tell stories because stories are ways of getting messages across that bypass the conscious mind, and therefore have more effect. This is one reason why we have been using stories, metaphors, and anecdotes throughout the book. Telling appropriate stories will make your presentation or training more entertaining, and people are more likely to remember you favourably as well.

Get a piece of paper and make a note of whatever stories come to mind now. Write down any key words, or a brief description that will act as a trigger for remembering the story. Make a note of the point of each story, because there must be some good reason for recalling it.

Here are some ideas that may help you come up with some stories.

Think about:

- What are the stories you tell other people?

Most people have stories they have recounted many times. Here are some examples:

- The stories you tell to your friends when you are chatting in the restaurant, around the barbecue, or just passing the time of day.
- The stories that come out when you are with your family – your parents, or your brothers and sisters – when you get together again and reminisce about the old days.
- The stories that you use when you first meet strangers and you start telling them about yourself.

They could be any events in your life that stand out in some way and have some kind of charge for you. These stories may be about:

- Your childhood – how you learned to do things, or misunderstood what adults were doing or talking about.
- Significant life events, such as starting school or a new job, when you got married, and so on.

- Events that happened on your holidays, when travelling, or being in foreign places.
- Crises that necessitated calling in specialists or tradespeople to fix things.
- Meetings with remarkable people.
- Anything at all: fact, fiction, or fantasy.

The stories don't have to be about your life. You can think of stories you have heard, or read in books. If you have young children, and you read them stories out loud, then you already have a good place to start. And if your parents read to you as a child, what would be some favourite stories that come to mind? Add these to your list as you remember them.

Collecting Stories

Become a collector of any stories that appeal to you. If you use this idea of collecting stories as a filter for your ongoing experience, you will soon have a repertoire of stories ready to put into your presentations and trainings as and when you need. And you will be able to choose the most appropriate story from your collection when you are putting together a training or presentation. So if you were asked to do a business presentation, you could select the best stories to tell your business audience, which would be excellent for getting certain points across.

Comedians using loops

A number of UK comedians use loops. For example, Ronnie Corbett, on The Two Ronnies, would sit in that big chair and tell a story or a joke, but not finish it, before going onto something else. And he would maybe do ten or 15 stories or jokes in a ten-minute sketch. Billy Connolly does it in his stage act. He starts a story, breaks it off, and keeps coming back to it all the way through his performance. Eddie Izzard also does this.

In the field of literature, the classic story using loops is *The Thousand and One Nights*, which is basically stories within stories within stories within stories . . . A modern writer who does this is

Garrison Keillor in his *Lake Wobegon* stories. Another prime example would be Tom Stoppard's radio play *Artist Descending a Staircase*, which consists of six nested loops, which are successive flashbacks. In fact, most plays and films are constructed in parallel sequences of short scenes. Usually, toward the end, the key characters and key storylines come together to resolve the plot. Over the centuries, little has changed in the structure of storytelling.

If you want to investigate some examples of how the theory of nested loops works, apart from what we are doing here, take a look at how other good storytellers do it: charismatic business presenters such as Tom Peters, or stand-up comedians, or whoever. Once you have this filter in place, you will discover how universal this practice is. Indeed, if you have ever done any computer programming, you will recognise this as similar to nesting subroutines.

Exercise 26: Nested Loops

Let's do an exercise using nested loops. In the last exercise, you put together five stories. For this exercise you need only three stories. Use your three best ones, knowing that you have two spares that you can use whenever you need them.

In your practice group, you will be presenting your three stories, in embedded metaphor form. This is what you do:

- Choose your three stories, and decide the order for telling them. You could choose a sequence that has some kind of flow, but this is not essential.
- For each story, consider: Where would be a good place to break this story? Find a place about three quarters of the way through, where you could stop one story and lead into the next.
- When you are ready, stand in front of your group, go into the trainer state, and so on, and begin telling your first story. And of course, you can use any of the non-verbal gestures, the Satir categories, that you think appropriate.

- Begin story #1, and when you are about three quarters of the way through, begin story #2. And then, when you are about three quarters of the way through that one, begin story #3. The break point is up to you, but you do need to have the audience engaged in the story before you break it off and start the next.
- If you were doing a full presentation or training, at this point, having left your third story, you would now start on the content of your presentation. But as this is the first time, you won't actually be putting any content in. When you get to the break point of story #3 just say, "Content", or, "Blah", or something to indicate that this is where the main part of your presentation would come. Or you could walk somewhere else on the stage, and then come back.
- When you have finished the content of your presentation, at the end of the training or presentation, go back to the nested stories, and come out of them in reverse order. In this exercise, resume the posture and the state you were in at the time you broke off story #3. Complete story #3, then story #2, and end with story #1.

If you really want to challenge yourself, you might want to find out what states you can elicit by telling each of the stories. Consider:

- Which state would story #1 elicit?
- Which state would story #2 elicit?
- Which state for story #3?

This is not something you have to do. Do it only if you want to challenge yourself. In fact, it might be interesting to discover if you can tell a story without eliciting a state. It would be a challenge to do this without eliciting states.

Do this exercise now in your group, and find out what happens for your audience when you tell your three nested stories.

Debrief

Although this exercise may seem to present quite a daunting task when you first think about it, when people actually do it, they often find that it is fun to do.

When you get to the point of re-entry into the stories, it is not necessary to give a brief résumé of where you were when you left off. You will find that the stories are most effective if you continue the story as though there had been no continuity break, as if you had never stopped. So you don't explain: "And getting back to the story that I told you about . . . " or, "You remember when we got to the point in the story where Arthur was just about to get hold of Excalibur . . . " you just stand in the same way, in the same location, and simply continue with the next line of the story. When you start off as if you had never stopped, people go straight back into the state they were in when you broke off the story earlier. You might notice a brief moment of confusion: "Where are we?" Then you will see them remember, "Ah, yes".

Transitions

You can either link the stories with a smooth transition, or you can break them quite abruptly, and make it very obvious that you haven't finished one story before starting another. For business presentations use the smooth transitions, where they move almost seamlessly one to the other. If you break a story abruptly and start another one, you will induce trance, because the conscious mind notices, "Hang on a minute, we haven't finished that story yet". The person is trying to put an ending on the story, yet you have already started another one, and that overloads the listener inducing yet a deeper level of trance, which might not be appropriate for business presentations – it depends what you are doing, and your intention. However, it could be particularly useful in personal development training.

Use relevant stories

The stories you use should be relevant to the context you are in, and to the content you are talking about. If you are using nested loops in a business presentation, then use business related stories. This is about matching the culture and the expectations of the people you are with. If you start telling them fairy tales or myths, unless you set things up very carefully, they might think you are behaving inappropriately for their 'serious-minded' organisation, and you will lose them. But it is very easy to retell a fairy tale in terms of a business story. All you do is change the superficial aspects – the characters and props – while keeping the basic plot – the action and what's at stake – the same.

We find that if people come into a room that is set up completely differently from what they expect, they automatically have to let go of all their preconceptions about the training. When they sit down they haven't a clue as to what was going to happen. That's a good position for you to be in, because it means they are now open to something new, something different.

So when you are confident in yourself, having done many trainings or presentations, then you feel free to experiment in what you do. Learn to play, and see what happens, knowing that if you do get a response you don't want, you can deal with it. Doing trainings and presentations is much more fun when you are flexible enough to turn any situation around to suit you.

Chapter Seventeen
Your Presentation

Let's add this piece to the overall scheme of things. When you are creating the structure of your presentation or training, this is what you do:

The Complete Structure of a Presentation or Training

Figure 17.1. The complete structure of a presentation

> *Little What* – overall frame
> *Why*
> Metaphor 1
>   Metaphor 2
>   Metaphor 3
>   *What*
>   *How*
>   (*What if*)
>   Metaphor 3
>   Metaphor 2
> Metaphor 1

- Start with the *little what*, to set a frame: "This is what the presentation or training is about." By establishing the frame the audience knows what to pay attention to.

- Give them the *why*: "This is why you would want to know this. This is why it is worth paying attention to this presentation."

Keep in mind that this *why* encompasses your audience's personal reasons, not your reasons. They may not have the same reasons as you, so you will have to guess what your audience's reasons are.

Before you go into the loops, you need to give the audience an overview of the presentation, and some reasons why they need to hear what you have to say, otherwise they will be wondering: "Why are you telling me all these stories?"

- Start Metaphor 1. If you are using three loops, then break off about three quarters of the way through the first story, and start Metaphor 2. Same thing: tell most of it, and then move into Metaphor 3. The three stories are now linked together.

- Give them the *what*, the content of the presentation, whatever it is you want to communicate to your audience.

- Do the *how*. You may want to run exercises, or you may want to tell people how they can use the information you have given them.

Then you have a choice:

- Either have your *what if* after the *how*, and then close your loops in reverse order: Metaphor 3, Metaphor 2, Metaphor 1,

- Or complete the three metaphors and then have the *what if*.

Your goal is to have an ending that leaves the audience in a high state. The decision about where to put the *what if* depends on your loops. If the last loop is a really strong close, one that would leave people in a very high state, either of amusement, or with a lot to think about, such as, "Wow. That's a completely different take on that. I've never thought of that before", then put the *what if* in after the *how*, and close on Metaphor 1.

If your Metaphor loops aren't designed to achieve that high state, because you have other reasons for the loops, then close the loops and do a final summation:

> "OK. If you were to learn and apply all of the things we have been talking about, these would be the consequences if you were to do that . . . And these would be the consequences of not doing it."

We use this structure for every presentation, of whatever length. If the training has modules, or a number of different segments to it, then we set a frame for the whole training with the introductory *what*. Then we do the *why* and the loops for the whole training. This all happens at the beginning of the first day. We will subsequently do a 4MAT for each segment of the training. And finally, when all the segments are done, we close the loops.

Leaving loops open

However, in most trainings neither of us will close every loop. We deliberately leave one or two loops open. The reason for this is that in teaching people NLP, we do not know where the boundaries are. As long as we have been teaching NLP, we have discovered that there is always more to learn. We are indebted to our students who have taught us so much that is so valuable over the years. In many disciplines, achieving mastery means that in a sense you start again with a 'beginner's mind'.

As master trainers, we realised how little we really knew about NLP, and it occurred to us that one of the biggest disservices we could ever do for someone would be to say, "You now know everything there is to know about this subject." Because we don't know everything: we don't know what the limits are, or even if there are limits. If people started thinking, "I know everything there is to know about that" then, essentially, we would have disempowered them. So by leaving the odd loop open, we leave some openness in the sense that there is always more to learn.

Chapter Eighteen
Putting It All Together

Now it's time to put it all together.

Exercise 27: The Final Presentation

This is when you put everything together for yourself. You have prepared some material for the content of your presentation. This may be anything you like. It could be something to do with your business, your career, or some part of the material that you normally present, that you want to restructure into this 4MAT system, or whatever.

This is the exercise:

- You are going to give the ten-minute presentation in front of your practice group. And you are going to structure it in the format outlined in *Figure 17.1*.
- Start with the overall frame, the *little what*.
- Then do the *why*: "This is what I am going to talk to you about. This is why you want to listen."
- Do your loops, just as you did in the last exercise. You can use the same loops, or different loops if you wish.
- Give the content of your presentation.
- If you are a trainer, and you are taking a segment of a training, don't get your group doing an exercise. If that is something you would normally do, just say, "Here is where I do the exercise, and this is the exercise I do". Pause. "Hi. Welcome back. So what did you learn, what did you discover . . . ?" Skip the actual exercise.
- If you are doing a business presentation, then you would probably want to tell them: "This is how you would use what I am talking about in your organisation or environment." Normally you wouldn't have an exercise in a business presentation, so you give them the *how*, verbally: "This is how you would use this."

- Then put in the *what if*, if that is the most appropriate place. Or put it in after closing your loops.
- Close your loops in the reverse order, as in the last exercise.

The only new thing here is the content. If you were wondering when you were going to put some content into your presentations, this is the time.

Having done all the previous exercises, this is just one more thing to add to what you can already do. As there is no way you can consciously track everything you have to do, you will have to let go and trust your unconscious mind. When you do that, it will all happen; you will be in control, responding to your audience, and taking them where you want to go.

Take ten minutes for your presentation – and please discipline yourself to keep to the ten minutes. The only thing to think about consciously is the outline. If you also do all the Satir categories unconsciously that is fine. If you use all the representational systems – visual, auditory, kinesthetic, auditory-digital – just go ahead and do that unconsciously. By now you will automatically be building rapport with the group, going into the trainer state, and all that. Just allow your unconscious mind to naturally do it for you anyway. And have some fun eliciting certain states in the audience – also unconsciously.

Do this final exercise now with your group. Take ten minutes each.

Debrief

So what did you learn, what did you discover, what questions do you have about putting everything together?

Many of the people doing this exercise during our trainings are surprised at how much they manage to integrate into their presentations. When we first did these exercises ourselves, one thing we became aware of – and you may have noticed this – is how much the other people improve over the training. When we thought about this we realised that the only way to notice that someone

232

else has improved is because you have made a similar level of improvement yourself, otherwise you wouldn't recognise it. So if you thought, "That person has really come on a long way. They've really transformed their whole presentation style through doing this", then take that as a sign that you have also progressed greatly in the course of this training.

Because we are always changing, it is not easy to evaluate where we are. It is possible to make comparisons with ourselves at an earlier time, but it is much easier to notice how someone else has changed and improved. You can notice that only in others, when you yourself have improved. Do you notice the improvements in the people in your practice group? That's a good indicator.

Use this Material

There is an important point about all the material you have learned in this book. We know these things work, because we are using them all the time. And they definitely work with any group. They will also work for you, but only if you use them. And the more you use them, the more they will become your own. You will know this has happened when you are doing a presentation, and you notice you are using these things unconsciously. They have become part of what you do, which means you will be presenting magically.

So take what you have been learning in this book, and do it for real. Test it out. You may want to start with some of the pieces, and then build up as you have more confidence. But the vital step is to go out there and do it, with the attitude: "I'm going to take a risk with it. And I am going to have fun!"

No matter what you do, no matter who you are, you have a very important message to put across to the people you are training or presenting to. When you are presenting magically, you will be getting your message across to all those people you are with, enabling them to transform as much as you have during the course in this book. This is what we think this is really about: you have expanded your own reality so that more things are now possible, and within it you are more flexible in what you can do.

Appendix A

How to Do This On Your Own

Working On Your Own

If you are interested in developing these skills, but you don't know anyone else around you who would also like to benefit from doing these exercises, then working through them on your own will work to an extent when you do the exercises in your imagination. However, it will not be enough. You do need to do things physically, to try out the different postures, and to actually speak the words, and so on. Mental rehearsal will definitely help, but the real learning comes from practising and getting feedback in front of an audience. Reading about the exercises will give you some background information, but you learn more than just intellectually when you get up to do a presentation.

If you are a presenter or trainer, and you are in front of groups of people on a regular basis, then tread carefully, and introduce one, maybe two things at a time into your regular trainings, so that you are adding new skills incrementally. For example, you may want to use the 4MAT system.

If you are a regular trainer and you are doing this alone it is better to have already practised so that:

- This time is not the first time you are using these techniques or this material.
- You know you can do them, and that they work,
- You have a sense that, "What I usually do in this situation is . . . "

Your Learning Style

If you have read Chapter Fourteen on the different learning styles, and you have identified that you have a *what if* learning style, it may appear to you that it is not so important for you to have done the exercises. You will have already been exploring alternatives, and taking each exercise out to the limit of what you can do with the information you have been given. But to have these behaviours installed in you, so that they occur automatically when you are training or presenting, then you do need to have done them beforehand.

Appendix B

Other Information

We run public trainings of *Presenting Magically*. Contact us for further information.

Contact Addresses:

* Contact David Shephard at
  The Performance Partnership
  web: www.performancepartnership.com

* Contact Tad James at
  Tad James Co.
  web: www.nlpcoaching.com

Bibliography

Atkinson, William Walker (1911). *Practical Mental Influence and Mental Fascination*, Illinois, USA: Yogi Publication Society.

Barbe, Walter B and Raymond H Swassing (1979). *Teaching Through Modality Strengths*, Ohio, USA: Zaner-Bloser.

Dumont, Theron Q (1914). *Advanced Course In Personal Magnetism*, Illinois, USA: Advanced Thought Publishing Co.

Dumont, Theron Q (1913). *The Art and Science of Personal Magnetism*, Illinois, USA: Advanced Thought Publishing Co.

Erickson, Milton H and Sidney Rosen (1982). *My Voice Will Go with You: The Teaching Tales of Milton H Erickson*, New York, USA: W W Norton.

Honey, Peter and Alan Mumford (1993). *The Manual of Learning Styles*, Maidenhead, UK: Peter Honey Publications.

Hutchison, Michael (1986). *Mega Brain: New Tools and Techniques for Brain Growth and Mind Expansion*, New York, USA: Beech Tree Books.

James, Tad (1997). *The Lost Secrets of Ancient Hawaiian Huna*, Volume 1, Hawaii, USA: Advanced Neuro Dynamics.

James, Tad and Wyatt Woodsmall (1988). *Time Line Therapy® and the Basis of Personality*, California, USA: Meta Publications.

James, Tad (2000). *Hypnosis: A Comprehensive Guide,* Carmarthen, UK: Crown House Publishing.

Jung, Carl (1991). *Psyche and Symbol* (translated by R F C Hull), Princeton, USA: Princeton University Press.

Korzybski, Alfred (1933). *Science and Sanity. An Introduction to Non-Aristotelian Systems and General Semantics*, Pennsylvania, USA: The International Non-Aristotelian Library Publishing Company.

Laborde, Genie (1998). *Influencing With Integrity*, Carmarthen, UK: Crown House Publishing.

Lankton, Stephen and Carol Lankton (1983). *The Answer Within: A Clinical Framework for Ericksonian Hypnotherapy*, New York, USA: Brunner/Mazel.

Lewis, Byron and Frank Pucelik (1990). *The Magic of NLP Demystified*, Oregon, USA: Metamorphous Press.

McCarthy, Bernice (1981). *The 4Mat System: Teaching to Learning Styles with Right/Left Mode Techniques*, Illinois, USA: Excel, Incorporated.

National Training Laboratories (1938). *Principles of Group Dynamics*.

Randall, Frank H (1901). *Your Mesmeric Forces and How to Develop Them*, London, UK: L N Fowler & Co.

Satir, Virginia (1978). *Peoplemaking*, California, USA: Science and Behavior Books.

Talbot, Michael (1987). *Beyond the Quantum*, New York, USA: Macmillan.

Talbot, Michael, (1991). *The Holographic Universe*, New York, USA: Harper Collins.

The Three Initiates (1912). *The Kybalion: A Study of the Hermetic Philosophy of Ancient Egypt and Greece*, Illinois, USA: Yogi Publishing Society.

Watzlawick, Paul (1976). *How Real is Real?: Confusion – Disinformation – Communication*, New York, USA: Random House.

Index

V

Visual,   15, 127, 130, 131, 132,
133, 134, 136, 140, 141, 142,
143, 149, 153, 154, 232
voice,   v, 28, 74, 75, 76, 77, 78, 79,
80, 81, 127, 136, 138, 139, 140,
141, 142, 143, 146, 147, 157,
158, 162, 164, 166, 168, 172,
173, 175, 212, 214, 239
voice intonation,   172, 175
voice tonality,   v, 74, 75, 80, 81,
127, 136, 138, 139, 141, 146,
147, 157, 166, 172, 173, 175

W

Wanton experimentation,   10,
43, 176
Women in the business
environment,   170
Woodsmall, Wyatt,   45, 239

CPSIA information can be obtained
at www.ICGtesting.com
Printed in the USA
BVHW041116210821
614355BV00004B/38